TWILIGHT

傍晚

TWILIGHT

A Contemporary Pastoral Poet of China

Zhang Lian

张联

Translated and with an introduction by

Keming Liu

Floating World Editions

First edition, 2022

Published by Floating World Editions,
26 Jack Corner Road, Warren, CT 06777

Translator and publisher acknowledge
and appreciate the contribution of the
Professional Staff Congress of the City
University of New York, whose reviewers
recognized the value of the project
and deemed it worthy of support.

Printed in the U.S.A.
ISBN 978-1-953225-02-3
Cataloguing-in-publication data is
available from the Library of Congress

Dedicated to my father . . .

Aboard the number 4 train to work on April 6, 2016, upon reading *The New York Times* article on Qing Ming, Tomb Sweeping Day in China, I silently cried, covering my face with tissue paper. Fumbling into my tote, I grabbed a pen and notepad to pour my thoughts into a poem dedicated to my father. Liu Tian Lu was killed by the Red Guards in 1968 when he was only forty-five years old, leaving mom with five of us ankle biters, me being the youngest. Today, I am older than my dad in 1968 and often wonder how my mom, forty at the time, handled all that sorrow and pressure on her own. Could I have been able to bear it? Compared to such tragedy, anything I encounter in life seems minuscule and of little significance.

My life source is a statistic
one of 1.5 million.
My life source is a particle
floating somewhere, nowhere.

Once a six-footer, army-trained
now a number, a puff of earth
in the vast smog-laden land
where the last seed he planted was me.

My life source, a particle, a number
will never witness his garden
where I grew, in his land and mine,
only that mine is smog free.

I can only breathe him through the particles
I can only mourn him as a number
I cannot show off his miraculous fruit
me, in an adopted land – my home.

献给父亲刘天禄

下面这首诗是在读完纽约时报登载的一篇有关中国清明节时重庆一处荒废的，无人问津的坟地。这里埋着文革时期被红卫兵打死的无辜受难者。坐在纽约南下的四号车上，我泪流满面，顾不上通行者们迷惑问津的神态，我拿出笔和纸匆匆写下这首献给父亲的诗：

我的生命源自一个数字
一百五十万之一。

我的生命来自一粒尘埃
漂游四处，漂流无处。

曾经高大正直，训练有素
如今则永远属于一个数字，一粒尘埃
游逛在雾霾重重的黄土大地
我胚胎的发源之处。

我生命之源，一个数字，一粒尘埃
将永不会目睹他培植的花园
我在他的园中成长，在他的国度和我的
只是我的有万里晴空。

如今我只能通过那无数的尘埃呼吸他
只能用数万之一来祭奠他，悼念他
我无法彰显他所创造的奇迹
我，在收养了我的国度 — 我今天的家园

Contents

Preface and Acknowledgments

This volume had an unlikely beginning, because I have always been suspicious of literary translation, especially between languages as dissimilar as Chinese and English, rooted in such disparate cultures. My stance was bolstered during my doctoral studies in linguistics at Columbia, when I embarked upon a cross-cultural analysis of text processing. Professor Clifford Hill provided examples of how children and adults process the same textual information so differently even within the same culture. He stressed that cultural schema affect the way people interpret texts. This research confirmed my doubts about translating Chinese literature into English or vice versa, a daunting task that requires deep familiarity with both cultures.

Then, without seeking translation work, two gigs somehow materialized. I was hired by ESPN to do simultaneous sports news in Mandarin and I also had a brief stint at the United Nations. My inadvertent journey toward this volume had begun.

Later, in 2004, the avant-garde theater director Robert Wilson staged an Asian-themed summer program featuring six Chinese visual artists-in-residence. I was enlisted to help translate discussions with these artists, who were invited to our house in Cutchogue for dumplings. We had a heated discussion of global art, music, and literature. While admitting that the visual arts and music have an easier time finding an international audience, they insisted that I take up the cause of bringing contemporary Chinese literature to English speaking readers.

With that encouragement, I made a selection of young Chinese poets, published in 2010 as *Voices of the Fourth Generation: China's Poets Today,* and added a critical introduction that spelled out my longstanding skepticism about literary translation. *Twilight* is the second volume of contemporary poetry I have translated. I was drawn to Zhang Lian's work, compelled by the backstory of a peasant with rudimentary education producing such powerful imagery and sure-handed lyricism. It helped that he lives in a region in Northwest China that was home to my ancestors. In 2018, I visited Zhang Lian and saw the cave home in which his family spent summers and winters with paltry sustenance from their land.

That landscape pulled me in emotionally and aesthetically. Growing up in cities further to the south (as well as Manhattan), I had never seen the vast prairies of northern China, where the clean, dry air opens your lungs and the endless horizon opens your eyes. It felt pure and free! After interviewing Zhang in his home library, I was taken by his scholarship and beautiful mind. I hope that my translation will foster that admiration as you pay a poetic visit to the vanishing landscape that Zhang Lian paints for us.

*　*　*

A literary collaboration as far-flung as this, beaming the dialogue between poet and translator from Manhattan to the edge of the Gobi desert, involves a support network with a global scope. On the Asian end, allow me to extend my heartfelt gratitude not only to the poet Zhang Lian, whose replies to my queries sometimes came in the dead of the night, but also to Mr. Xuejun Zhao (赵学军), without whom I would not have had the chance to reach the poet and conduct the numerous interviews with him during the translation process. I am indebted to Mr. Jianfei Ma (马剑飞), Yong Wang (王甬), Jiangwei Liu (刘江伟), and many others at the Beijing headquarters of China's International Education Exchange Program. Their encouragement gave me the heart to continue and offered a source of pride in the important work they do internationally to foster the understanding of Chinese culture.

I would be remiss if I did not mention Mr. Yongzan Xu (徐永赞), Vice President of Hebei University of Science and Technology, who offered selfless support for my research in China and seamlessly arranged my voyage to Zhang Lian's village. What would have been an arduous trek not long ago became a memorable 24-hour experience.

I express my gratitude to PSC-CUNY for its continued support of diversity in scholarship. Without its funding, much of the field research would not have been possible. My sincere appreciation and thanks go to Peter Thompson, editor of *Ezra*, whose enthusiasm for my translated poetry carried me through years of doubt and more than a few setbacks in completing this volume.

Speaking of perceptive editors, for the second time in my career it has been a joy to work with Ray Furse, editorial director of Floating World Editions, an independent publisher that has distinguished itself over the years for its commitment to Asian thought and literature. His deft editorial hand, and his belief in the significance of the daring project of discovering a new poet from the remote reaches of China's hinterland, shine in a publishing world more and more fixated on easily sold books that follow conventional formulae for success. I thank him for his faith in me, and salute him for his intrepid intellectual strength.

When a hometown library is the source of comfort, peace, resources, and kindness, the writer ought to gratefully acknowledge such a gift. The Cutchogue New Suffolk Free Library is a scholar's refuge and a community gem, where the director, Rosemary Winters, her colleagues Dawn Manwaring, Darlene Brush, Seth Bank and many others, have been the foundation supporting my work. I secluded myself for hours on the second floor, devouring not only the excellent collection but also the speedily delivered interlibrary loans that fueled this project's completion.

I am grateful to my husband, Charles A. Riley, who was always there when I needed spiritual and intellectual support and who attended each ramification of my widely ranging thoughts during the translation of the poems.

Finally, I appreciate the steadfast friendship that I received from James Lee and Mary Chen-xiao Lee. Their kindness and respect for my endeavors reinforced my belief in my task and pushed me to pursue every challenging detail as I completed this volume. Special thanks should also go to my colleague and poet, Linda Jackson, whose valuable feedback is deeply appreciated, as well as to Yizhen Zhao, who lent her well-read eyes and impressive mastery of Chinese classics to the manuscript in its early stage.

I am dedicating this book to my father, a dignified and brave intellectual and translator, who never lived to see my achievements. He was killed by the Red Guards at the start of the Cultural Revolution.

Keming Liu
December 8, 2021
Cutchouge, NY

Zhang Lian
and the
New Chinese Pastoral

Visit to a Poet

The highland air envelops me as I descend from car 16 of the Beijing–Ningxia Silk Road Express. Jostled awake by a brisk tug at my feet, I hear the conductor announce in a hushed tone, *Yanchi jiuyao daole!* (Yanchi stop soon!). My Silk Road voyage began with an overnight train that traverses China's northern terrain from east to west, passing through the ancient capital of Xi'an. The

Express train from Beijing to Ningxia.

rhythmic chugging of the wheels had lulled me into a sound sleep under the fresh, starched linen sheet, which shortened the trip to a couple of dreams that had evaporated from my head by the time of my arrival. Jumping off the upper bunk, I grabbed my luggage tucked under the lower bed and headed toward the exit, half awake.

A wispy blanket of morning mist hovers over the spare platform as I step off the train at this rural backwater en route

City gate of Yanchi.

2

to Yinchuan, the capital of Ningxia Hui Autonomous Region in northwest China, bordering Inner Mongolia along a bend of the Yellow River. I am greeted by the instant coolness of the steppe air mixed with that sweet, earthy smell of the alluvial plains.

Yanchi (盐池) sits at the crossroads of three provinces: Shaanxi to the east, Gansu to the south, Inner Mongolia to the north. It rests on the southern edge of the Ordos steppe that meets central China's loess plateau, enabling a half-farming, half-herding lifestyle. The Great Wall cuts through its northern border with Inner Mongolia, which is a mere stone's throw from a county wall that was fortified with a new tower in 2016 over the ruins of the old wall erected in 1443. With a population of 160,000, the township originally housed ethnic Tibetans, Mongols, and Muslims whose livelihood depended on herding. In 241 and 211 BCE Emperor Qin staged two migrations culminating in a total of several hundreds of thousands of Han people flooding into the region.

Ningxia today is officially an "autonomous region," allowing ethnic groups to preserve their cultural and religious practices under the close supervision of the central government. Only 66.4 miles long and 42 miles wide, Yanchi is today one of its poorest counties. Slated for organized internal migration by the government's five-year plan, some 63,000 residents have already been relocated to a Levittown-like development thousands of miles away, uprooting families that have farmed the region for centuries. My visit to the poet Zhang Lian (张联, b. 1967) allowed me to see firsthand the last traces of a way of life that had endured for millennia.

The station platform was laid with cobblestones, so each step tugged at the wheels of my luggage. I lifted the bag and took off down the stairs. Like the passageways in the New York City subway system, I was soon navigating the dank underground, first across, then up and down, and finally to the exit. A small crowd was gathered at the turnstiles and some were hollering for rides. The few cab drivers were soon snatched up by the passengers at this early hour and I could not see my driver or my host. I doubled back to the station to ask a security guard if this station was indeed Yanchi and where my pickup would be waiting. "Exit the station and to your left is the waiting room.

Convening in Zhang Lian's living room-classroom.

Wait there." As I rolled my luggage through the turnstile, someone tapped me on the shoulder. "Professor Liu?" I turned to face a short man in his fifties beaming a smile. Behind him was another short man whose face I recognized immediately as the poet's. *Xinku la, xinku la* (Hard journey, hard journey), Zhang Lian repeated. "Not so bad," I replied. The faint, vaporous light of dawn was quickly replaced by a greyish blue sky as we drove into the county center.

Zhang Lian appeared like the shepherd and farmer he had long been, solidly built with a square jaw and large hands thick from years of labor. He wore a boyish crop cut of hair, black polo shirt under a blue windbreaker, black pants matching the polo shirt, and black leather shoes to mark the occasion.

By six AM three of us, including Zhang's wife Mao Hong-ye (毛红叶) were sitting around a small table in Zhang's living room

The poet taking pictures.

that doubles as his writing classroom, where a dozen children come for after-school tutoring. In the 20-by-40 foot space, half of the long side wall is decked with a sturdy bookshelf filled with Chinese history and literature texts. Separated by a doorway in the middle of the wall, the other half of the side wall is occupied by calligraphy scrolls of Zhang's poems. As I scanned the room, I noticed calligraphy carved into each door panel and remarked on the richness of literary ornament. "Each door panel is carved with a *Twilight* poem," the poet explained, demurely. They are all here in the volume you are holding. Zhang's love of poetry was obvious and infectious.

Zhang Lian's literary refuge was a stark contrast to its surroundings. The thin, dry layer of the loess soil, at an elevation of four thousand feet that sees an average annual precipitation of just 4.8 inches, makes farming incredibly difficult. The most rain falls during the months of July and August. Until the late 1970s, people were still living in *yaodong,* simple cave homes dug out of the loess. The caves are cool in summer and warm in winter. Yanchi is marked by the tail end of the Great Wall, a tamped earth structure built to keep invaders at bay. The remnants of the wall can be seen still, some parts dating to the seventh century BCE. Over the millennia, parts have crumbled, leaving tree-stump like protrusions mixed with newly planted saplings and shrubs, part of a central government effort to reclaim the grassland. To preserve cultural relics, the central government pumped in over a billion yuan ($154 million) to rebuild part of the wall by layering over the stumps with gray brick, matching the look of Beijing's Great Wall. The result is a mile-long elevated wall walk with watch towers along the Mongolian border at the edge of town. The day I was visiting, I spotted exercise buffs climbing the steps and running or walking briskly in the clear, clean air, a rare treat in China. The government effort to rebuild Yanchi is part of the One Belt and One Road Initiative. Yanchi sits at the mouth of the ancient Silk Road, an important strategic frontier. Ironically, having been built to keep the barbarians out, the Great Wall is now welcoming foreign funds and tourists to keep it standing.

Traditional Chinese culture favors rootedness to the cropland, but Yanchi's topography defies reliance on crops alone.

Cave home cut into the loess.

Remnants of the Great Wall nearby.

The steppes are ideal for grazing so most farmers here have adopted a semi-nomadic lifestyle, herding but returning to their home base instead of setting up seasonal tent camps. Given its unique topography, vast grazing plateau, hills and deserts, a tight-knit society of farmers emerged who own not only small plots of land but also livestock such as Tan-yang, a species of prized sheep whose meat is tender and fleece soft. Zhang Lian grew up farming sunflowers and herding sheep.

Later that same morning, Zhang Lian's home became crowded with friends invited to accompany us to Zhang's home village of Little Sunny Ditch (Xiao Yang Gou, 小阳沟), some twenty minutes away by car. Before we got on the road, the group took me first to a local *Tan-yang ge le* eatery, a small family-owned restaurant that serves a specialty buckwheat noodle soup locally known as *ge le*. The ingredients come in separate bowls, one small bowl of lamb stock peppered with spice, cilantro, and delicious buttery lamb meat pieces and a large bowl in the middle of the table filled with *ge le* submerged in clear cool water to keep them *al dente*. I dished the noodles out of the big bowl and transferred them into my spicy base. I slurped like the others with delight and soon found that I wanted more. A second bowl of *ge le* arrived and it was gone instantly.

The group of men was pleased to see a city girl eating like a truck driver. The ice was broken straightaway.

Bowls of buckwheat noodle soup, *ge le*.

With laughter and full bellies, we drove out on National Highway 307, which runs parallel to the Silk Road Rail Line. It's a two-way, single lane highway. We saw no oncoming or passing cars during the drive to Little Sunny Ditch. Aside from remnants of the Great Wall, I saw vast, empty prairies with no trees, just an endless expanse of grassland. I was curious why the locals are not making use of the land for farming. My companions in the car, Zhang Lian, Mr. Bai the Cultural Ministry Historian and Chairman, the driver, also a poet, and Mr. Mao, Zhang Lian's brother-in-law, a government administrator, all piped up saying that China's central government had installed a no-farming policy to revive the depleted pastures and preserve the environment. As they were talking, I spotted ahead of us on both sides of the road vast fields of solar panels, beyond which was a stretch of

The translator stands beside fields of solar panels along the road.

The lonely village road by Little Sunny Ditch.

wind turbines. I was told these sustainable solar and wind resources provided power for the neighboring megacities and townships for domestic use, irrigation, and industry.

Ten minutes after passing the renewable energy fields, I spotted a scattering of one-story brick and mud houses. "Here's my village, Little Sunny Ditch!" Zhang Lian cheerfully informed me. The unmarked village borders a narrow and straight tar-paved road that was recently built as part of One Belt One Road.

Presently, the road comes to a sudden stop just over the horizon, where there are no more inhabitants, only the Mongolian desert lying beyond. It stretches into the Ordos desert a couple hundred miles away. The cool April breeze blowing in from the north dries your throat instantly. The site is so remote and barren that it attracts no tourists. This is where the poet Zhang Lian lived and wrote all these years, where the vast expanse of

Zhang Lian's village today.

8

Zhang Lian's old garage in Little Sunny Ditch.

emptiness, blue sky above, yellow earth below, and a dark road cutting right through it reminds one of a Rothko painting.

We veered off the highway and onto the paved road into the village, a cluster of houses with some chickens pecking in the field and not a soul to be seen. Zhang's brick home is set in a courtyard encircled by a tamped-earth wall that leaves an opening wide enough for a cart to get through alongside a mud kitchen with broken windows. A tin door protects another mud structure that used to be the garage for his two-wheeled hand cart and later a motorized, three-wheeled cart used to transport crops to the nearest town or for taking his two children for a ride. In the middle of the yard is a patch of cracked earth, a humble vegetable garden that his father tends daily. The courtyard is off the narrow, paved village road but it is safe to say that there is no worry about traffic keeping one awake at night. On the other side of the road

The kitchen with broken windows by the courtyard gate, with garage to the left.

9

The shallow bank of the Little Sunny Ditch.

One of the wells Zhang Lian dug in the eighties.

on the vast prairie of the Mongolian steppe, Zhang's family cemetery holds his mother and other ancestors, each marked only by a mound of earth. Off the cemetery is a jagged stretch of ravine from which the village got its name. Before it was renamed, it was called Little Shadow Ditch, which to me seemed more accurate as I saw no sun penetrating its depths, carved by rainwater and erosion. A period of continuous drought caused the villagers to think that "shadow" was an inauspicious name so they changed it to "sunny" in an attempt to bring back the much-needed blessing of water. On the day I was there, the sun was warm and the air clear. There was no sign of any dampness as the ground was baked dry. The straight narrow road cuts through the prairie to the horizon's edge where the sky meets the steppes.

In the 1980s, when drought made growing anything impossible, the government launched a campaign to lift the villagers out of poverty by requiring each family to dig two wells, a movement dubbed the Mother Well Project. Each well was mandated to provide close to 3,000 cubic feet of water, with two such wells sustaining a family of four for the year. Each well would take four persons over ten days to complete. It was a Herculean effort on the part of the peasants, who owned only a handful of shovels. Zhang Lian and his brothers and cousins would daily descend the hand-operated crank cable to work in the dark underground and basket by basket transport dirt to the surface. One morning, Zhang Lian rose early to get to the then 23-foot deep well. Two hours passed and the sky started to crack open and the sunlight told Zhang it was breakfast time. When he attempted to shinny up the cable, he realized that he had made a mistake in coming down. The crank was no longer working. Zhang mustered his remaining strength to climb up, dripping sweat the whole way, only to fall right down to the bottom. With no mobile phone, no cry loud enough for anyone to hear him, his instinct to survive kicked in and up he went like a mountain climber. When he finally emerged, he collapsed by the opening of the well without the strength to move. I walked around the well, his cave home, and the yard several times in an attempt to absorb the magnitude of the hardship these herders endured in the days when I was growing up in a city and enjoying a carefree college campus life. I could not help appreciating Zhang's writing all the more.

Contemplating this hard-scrabble existence, I slipped into a reverie. Directly, I realized that my companions were scattered in the field, some smoking, some staring into the distance. Zhang Lian stood by smiling. "Should I pay a visit to your father?" I

Zhang Lian's father sitting under a date tree, planting a few scallions in the backyard.

suggested. With a hand wave from Zhang, everyone came running and we went together to pay respects to the paterfamilias in his brick, single-level, three-room house built by one of Zhang's brothers. Through the door, one enters a space with two more doors, one on each side, that lead to the other rooms. On the center wall hangs a portrait of Zhang's late mother. Chinese filial piety dictates that a family display its ancestral portraits at all times and set up an altar with fruits and daily hot meals during major festivals. Offspring bow to their ancestors

The gate through which Zhang Lian gazed into the changing colors of twilight.

for protection, good health, and prosperity, and send the spirits off with good wishes and a full stomach.

Under the gaze of Zhang's mother I greeted Zhang's father, who stood leaning against the threshold of the side door, holding a cane, slightly bent over in an old-fashioned Chinese tunic that I saw my grandmother wear when I was a little girl. The androgynous style was fashioned so tailors could make dozens at a time for men and women alike, a Chinese prêt-à-porter innovation. We talked for a few minutes, but I couldn't make out a syllable of what he was trying to tell me in his thick regional dialect. Later as we strolled up the pasture and around the ditch where water used to flow, Zhang Lian related that his father was lamenting that no one wanted to stay in the village and how quiet it was. But he would never move away.

I inspected the courtyard. The tamped-earth structure of the kitchen is still standing, its doors tightly shut. Between the kitchen outbuilding and the main brick house is the gate from which Zhang Lian often observed the setting sun. It figures in many of the poems in this volume. "I know what time it is by the angle of the sun," Zhang said. "And each movement marks the distance it has just traveled over the pasture." When Zhang was herding sheep homeward, he marked the setting sun closely to gauge the distance and time left to travel. He started to imagine the world more freely, the color of the sky, and the fantasy led him to ponder his own existence. The daily pilgrimage resulted in his *Twilight* project of over three thousand poems and still counting.

There were hints of a refreshing rural naiveté among the group that accompanied me to Little Sunny Ditch. I felt an instant bond with these men and women, who gathered at our lunch table after we returned to Yanchi. I was able to trust each and every folklore guru, their wives and children. That sense of the guardedness we are so accustomed to assume evaporated and we were all ourselves, without pretense or boasting, just sharing laughter and joy. To welcome me, each one at the table stood up to recite a poem, long ones, from the Tang and Song dynasties, to sing a local song, and to toast *ganbei*, "bottoms up." One young man whose last name is Zuo (*zuo* also means "left," appropriate for his avid devotion to Maoist ideals) brought Mao pins made during the Cultural Revolution as gifts for each of us. He is a member of the National Red Club, which hosts their annual Red Collections Exchange Summit when members barter, exchange, and buy revolutionary mementos for their small shops scattered all over China, and to reminisce about the "good old days." Strangely enough, there is now a feverish revival of nationalism in China as a result of the country's fast dash toward modernization, creating many of the world's billionaires but at the same time leaving in its wake desolate villages and forsaken locals, too poor and illiterate to move anywhere. To these lower-class citizens, Mao remains a revered leader, the "Great Helmsman" who safeguarded Chinese tradition. Ironically, they fail to fathom the level of devastation Mao's policies wreaked and how anyone sitting at the table of a poet would have been a target of his anti-intellectual purges. The lunch crowd dispersed with the young man bellowing, Elvis Presley style, "Sailing the sea depends on the helmsman, life and growth depend on the sun, rain and dew drops nourish the crops, waging revolution depends on Mao Zedong thought . . ."

Zhang Lian and Twilight

Precise place of origin is of the utmost importance for all Chinese. To identify Zhang simply as Chinese, or even from Ningxia province, would not do justice to the specific locale from which his most haunting poetic lines emerged. It is the characteristics of the region that shaped the literary achievement of a desperate farmer and shepherd. Zhang wrote his first notable poem on New Year's Eve in 2001 upon returning from a street market twenty kilometers from his home village in one of the poorest counties in China. With its barren soil and deforested mountains, the region has been identified by the United Nations as one of the least inhabitable zones in the world. Ironically, it has produced a cadre of noted writers, now collectively credited as the XiHaiGu (西海固) school, after the abbreviated name of the region, which includes the administrative districts of Xiji, Haiyuan, and Guyuan. XiHaiGu literature offers a raw depiction of ordinary lives complicated by innately human tragedies, either caused by nature or self-inflicted. An earthy atmosphere, rural imagery, and unmistakably folk-country style infuse the story lines. Through the region's looking glass, we glimpse the frayed moral fabric of the hyper-capitalist country that is today's China. The authenticity of Zhang's voice comes from real experience.

Yanchi is a county of villages inside which small hamlets are home to close-knit families. Zhang lived in the Wang Family Well village, which encompasses the small hamlet of Little Sunny Ditch. Perhaps the Wang family allowed one of its daughters to marry a young man in a nearby village with the last name of Zhang. When that marriage gave birth to a boy, he brought his last name to Little Sunny Ditch, where only thirty families eke out a meager living from the dry land.

The third child of four, Zhang Lian completed his middle school education in 1983. Neither of his parents had any formal education but his father taught himself to read and write and served as the hamlet's bookkeeper and community leader. His love for classical Chinese operas fanned his interest in reading, a legacy he passed down to Zhang Lian. The poet's memory begins with a traumatic national event, the death of Mao Zedong in 1976, when Zhang Lian was nine. His father had purchased a small radio two years before, a luxury item in the countryside. The whole village nestled around the little magic box to listen to the continuous dirge of the mourning music and reports of politicians from near and far paying last respects. The country came to a stop as far as production or labor and everyone was engaged in making wreaths and setting up shrines with large Mao portraits surrounded by paper flowers, home-made cakes, fruits and candies, to honor the passing of the "savior of modern China." Zhang Lian's heart was heavy with the loss of the Helmsman and he was determined to make good use of his mind to change his lot.

The Wang's Happy Well Village School was over six miles from Little Sunny Ditch so Zhang Lian and other kids boarded there, returning home on Fridays on foot. As a little boy, Zhang was sickly from lack of adequate nutrition and the weekly round trip became a training regimen for sustained leg power and his later herding career. Zhang did not experience city life until 1992, when he followed his father and two brothers on a day-long trip of 148 kilometers to Wuzhong city. The big, noisy urban center left him feeling scared and lacking control. The outside world, he surmised, was better avoided. After graduation from middle school, Zhang Lian stayed in the village from 1988 to 1993, substitute teaching at an elementary school, earning eight yuan, about one dollar, per month. For five years he taught the children, bought books with his paltry earnings, and wrote poetry on the flip side of his students' discarded exercise papers. In 1993, he moved back to his hamlet where he started farming 2.5 hectares of land, growing potatoes and sun-

Zhang Lian at Little Sunny Ditch

flowers, crops that could withstand drought, and raising sheep. In a good year when rainfall was abundant, his crops could barely sustain the family of four.

Zhang Lian is the only one of four siblings (he has older and younger brothers, and an older sister), who remained in his home village to learn farming from his father. The story of how he became a poet is dramatic. In 2000 and 2001, a severe drought devastated Zhang's crop. Desperate to provide a "sumptuous" New Year's dinner and a package of candy for his seven-year-old son, Zhang trudged to the street fair twenty kilometers from home with an old sheepskin, the last item of value he owned. Humiliated and embarrassed when it went unsold, Zhang dragged his feet home in the wintry cold and scribbled the lines of the draft of his first major poem, "I Trudge with My Skin in My Hand" (p. 49). "I felt I was walking with my skin peeled off and all my flesh exposed," confessed Zhang in an interview with a Chinese journalist. Writing was his only hope and also provided a source of spiritual solace.

I trudge with my skin in my hand
among the rich crowd, owning not a penny
entering the cacophonous market.
I plod with my skin in my hand, no energy to take in the
world
among the rich crowd,
dragging a crushed heart.
I cannot stop to explore, or to take a rest.
I own not a stool, no place to put up my feet.
I slog with my skin in my hand
no desire to sell out my soul.
But a truck loaded with smile
crowded to the brim with beautiful clothes and New Year's
goods!
A soul is crushed flat today.
To where can I flee? Even a speck of dust has to return to
the ground.

Since then, Zhang has composed over three thousand poems, scribbled on the margins of used textbooks, old magazines, and

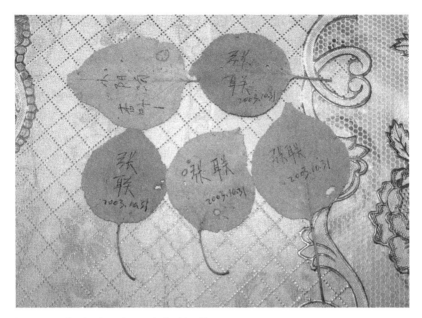
Leaves collected and annotated by Zhang.

newspapers. When he was in the mood, he would also grab some dry leaves and inscribe them with his name and the date as well as his village name. The morning I was at his home, he pulled several books off the shelf and spread them over the desk that doubles as a dining table. Nestled in the pages of his poetry collection are leaves with dates, locations, and the names of the plants from which those leaves had fallen. Some dates correspond to the poems composed on the days he picked up the leaves.

Just another farmer in Little Sunny Ditch, Zhang and his family lived in a three-room, flat-roofed, dwelling by the caves in which he grew up. They owned a few chickens, a pig, a shabby shed, a two-handled farm cart. Neighbors considered him a dilettante farmer who failed to focus on his proper duties. In 2001, after completing several hundred poems under the heading *Twilight,* Zhang borrowed money to pay for printing them as a book. Little known in his home village where literacy remained at middle school level, Zhang Lian was ironically on the cusp of discovery by literati in the distant capital, Beijing.

In 2005, Zhang Lian boldly abandoned his farm work and devoted his life to writing poetry and running a bookstore in his village. He sells books and operates a tutorial service for local school children. Located on Main Street, sandwiched between a noisy thoroughfare where all kinds of vehicles blast by and a back street where vendors sell fruits and vegetables, the bookstore is flanked with rickety bookshelves against two walls with three rows of desks and chairs in the middle to accommodate children who spend time studying.

As the founder of the Grassroots Poetry Tribe (草根诗歌部落) established in 2016, Zhang Lian started a movement in Chinese contemporary literature by defying the stigma of being a mere farmer. As the first farmer-poet without educational credentials to be inducted into the elite Writers Association, Zhang Lian felt it his mission to support poets of similar backgrounds. His Grassroots Poetry Tribe aims to promote poetics originating from nature, with a focus on the natural ecological order. Through promoting country poets, Zhang Lian attempts to highlight the importance of such writers, who are often neglected by mainstream literary circles. *The Tribe* has published many volumes of farmer-poets' works and won wide acclaim and media coverage since its inception.

Much of the Chinese poetic tradition has been defined by its famed Tang and Song poetry into which Zhang fits only loosely. Few contemporary writers are known to the West except for Bei Dao, the Misty Poets[1] representative, or Mo Yan, the recent Nobel Prize recipient and novelist. A world viewed through the lens of a farmer enjoys that unadorned, intuitive beauty. Zhang's lyrical skills depend on the understated, everyday vernacular through which he expresses his raw observation of daily encounters with nature. Over two hundred poems from his *Twilight* collection were translated into Japanese and published in the journal *Blue* in 2005. Now an English-speaking audience will make his acquaintance.

---

[1] "Misty Poets" (Menglong Shiren, 朦胧诗人) is a group that emerged in the late 1970s and 1980s. Their poetry is marked with abstract language and obscure meaning that eludes uniform interpretation. Influenced by Western philosophy literature, and imagery techniques, the Misty Poets eschewed social realism in pursuit of esoteric metaphors and rich imagery. Writers in this school made candid social commentaries and indulged in expressing veiled political viewpoints.

In 2008, the Chinese Writers Association accepted Zhang into their elite circle. As the first member without a college degree, and the first and only farmer-poet inducted, Zhang entered a realm that had been dominated by educated, trained professionals who toed a tight line to the tradition.

The XiHaiGu School of Farmer-Writers

The southern counties of Ningxia province from which the school's name is derived—Xiji, Haiyuan, and Guyuan—are some of the poorest in the nation. The barren and rugged topography, cold and dry winters and hot summers compound the harsh lives of the farmers eking out a living there. In a good year, with rainfall abundant enough to grow potatoes and sunflowers,  a farmer makes less than $500. A surprising response to this harsh reality has been resorting to words to describe it. Most of the farmer-writers associated with the group barely finished high school. With little more than used textbooks as writing pads, they are turning some of the most touching moments of their experiences into gut-wrenching texts that are gaining a broad audience in China.

Zhang Lian is typical of the new breed. On March 16, 2010, he was recognized as one of the top ten rural poets at an award ceremony held in Sichuan province, a harbinger of the 2012 Nobel Prize recognition of Mo Yan, a farmer during his teens and the son of farmers in rural Shandong who went on to become an internationally known novelist.

Zhang Lian is aware of the trendy city life outside his village and the more lucrative businesses he could pursue. He prefers to devote his energy to books and writing. Zhang confesses that he reads profusely to quench his thirst for outside information and poetic inspiration. Almost by chance, he landed on Charles Baudelaire's "Chacun Sa Chimère" ("To Each His Own Chimera") which reads: "These grave and weary faces showed no evidence of despair. Beneath the splenetic cupola of the heavens, their feet trudging through the dust of an earth as desolate as the sky, they journeyed onwards with the resigned faces of men condemned to hope for ever." Riffing on Baudelaire's imagery, Zhang poured out his own suspended despair in "The Hunchbacks" (p. 47).

> Under heaven
> a few hunchbacks
> are entering the village.
> In the gentle touch of dark blue
> the village is moving;
> the dark blue sky
> the dark blue twilight
> the dark blue tree branches
> the dark blue people
> the dark blue houses.
> In the tree branches by a house
> a touch of red, moving
> carrying with it peacefulness
> and a few hunchbacked men.

Here the poet presents the Sisyphean paradox of a farmhand's toil. "Day in and day out, my village farmers go out to collect hay and herbs to eke out a meager living," Zhang says in his response to my query about the bent figures in this poem. They trudge to the fields daily, weighed down by the heavy sacks of herbs and hay collected to barter for food, sugar, and salt. They continue to hope without ever doubting. The persistent spirit of the hard-working peasants, the literal backbone of China, offers a sharp contrast to the frenzied city life where billions are transacted, funneled into shadow banking, or lavished on shopping for luxury brands.

Zhang Lian's writing represents a trend to a return to nature, and he has been aptly dubbed *dāngdài yuánshēngtài zìrán zhǔyì shīrén* (当代原生态自然主义诗人), loosely translated "poet of contemporary ecological naturalism." Zhang does not put soliloquies or philosophical speeches into his everyday voice. His lines are the peasants' daily thoughts and "mundane" concerns expressed in a realistic tone, but with explicit belief in a superpower that he calls the "divine realm." It is in this "imagined supernatural realm" *(huanxiang de jingjie,* 幻想的境界) that Zhang Lian is sustained, by words and uncluttered peace, when reality keeps him awake.

The poem "Insomnia" (p. 93) offers a good introduction to Zhang's metaphorical method. Longing for protection is transformed into an image of his mother, with whom the child's only chore is to eat and sleep, and of course grow. Pressed for an autobiographical note on this poem, he told me: "The 'you' in the poem is my mom. I did not succeed in placing my soul back into her bosom in the cross pollination of reality and spirit along with the entire universe and the significant God. It was to express a genuine loneliness, which I wish to stress and reveal to God, like a child's sad call for help. It is the testimony of a child's pure longing on the real and imagined country road."

My insomnia
keeps my night oil burning
when reaching the thought of twilight
I spot a shadow rolling by the gate.
I run after it
to face a big ball of cotton sheet
like a sail
stranded at the pigsty.
The setting sun is still wearing a bit of yellow hair
yet I failed to notice your homecoming
return.
Twilight follows me into my hut
accompanying the lonely flickering flame
in an everlasting wintry day.

Zhang Lian once confided, "I love writing even though it does not make money." When he was a child, his father once dragged him twenty kilometers to the nearest hospital on a wooden plank when he was suffering from acute hepatitis. The memory still informs his art. On a bumpy country road, gusts of wind woke the sick boy and he had a hallucination of a pink-tinged horizon blanketing the land with a reddish hue. "It was sad, but magnificently beautiful," he said. He later recast the scene in the poem, "The World Pulls Down Its Curtain Here" (p. 42).

My coal truck passed by your village
one evening.
When the sun burned red
mounting a patch of gorgeous splendor.
Glowing lake
cloud ablaze
passing through the patchy elm trees
I think of you again.
For this patch of glorious color,
you must be heading out, I conjecture,
to embrace the magical light.
The world's dusk
pulls down its curtain here
and my heart is reluctant to depart.

What typifies this school of rustic writers, whose most famous exponent is the novelist and Nobel laureate Mo Yan, is the new direction their realism takes. "For a very long time Chinese realism was of a socialist realist persuasion, so it had to be filled with ideological and political messages," comments Michel Hocks, professor of Chinese in the School of Oriental and African Studies at the University of London.[2] The stories and poetry of this new school offer matter-of-fact narration from the eye of an everyday person going through life's daily routine. Instead of featuring revolutionary superheroes as dictated by socialist realism, XiHaiGu writers fill their works with real characters set in rural China where mundane things happen, even though

[2] Andrew Jacobs and Sarah Lyall, "After Past Fury for Peace Prize, China Embraces Nobel Choice," *The New York Times,* 12 October 2012.

the plot sometimes skews toward mythology or fairy tales. The Nobel Prize committee observed, "Through a mixture of fantasy and reality, historical and social perspectives, Mo Yan has created a world reminiscent in its complexity of those in the writings of William Faulkner and Gabriel Garcia Marquez, at the same time finding a departure point in old Chinese literature and in oral tradition."[3]

Another attribute of the XiHaiGu School is its proud assertion of their "otherness" in a modernizing country where poor farmers endure persona-non-grata status. In a wealth-driven society, these farmers are viewed as backward illiterates, condemned to poverty as their birthright. They are the "other," beyond the city limits in the eyes of the prosperous bureaucrats, entrepreneurs, and the notorious princelings descended from Chinese politicians. According to Homi K. Bhabha, the Chinese farmer-writers, not unlike characters in V.S. Naipaul's fiction, exhibit an ability to "forbear their despair, to work through their anxieties and alienations towards a life that may be radically incomplete but continues to be intricately communitarian, busy with activity, noisy with stories, garrulous with grotesquerie, gossip, humor, aspirations, fantasies."[4] They are "signs of a culture of survival that emerges from the other side" of the dominant enterprise. The centrifuge of China's literary tradition spins out writers who are off-center and whose works are passed over by editors of anthologies, especially those compiled in the West. Similar to subjects in colonies, the Chinese farmers are defined by urban arbiters who have written and spoken *for* them, if they acknowledge them at all. Now for the first time in modern China's literary history, the "other" has chosen to speak on its own behalf, taking pride in being marginal, accepting and celebrating otherness the same way as Edward Said characterized African and Caribbean writers, who by asserting themselves accepted and celebrated their blackness.[5]

---

[3] Per Wästberg, Presentation Speech for the 2012 Nobel Prize in Literature, Stockholm Concert Hall, December 12, 2012.

[4] Homi K. Bhabha, *The Location of Culture* (New York: Routledge, 1994), p. xiii.

[5] Edward W. Said, "The Politics of Knowledge." *Raritan* II: I (Summer 1991), p. 22.

The analogy with the Chinese farmer-writers is not far-fetched if one understands the seemingly homogeneous culture of China where prejudice is openly displayed, especially in major cities. Though zip codes may not readily identify the haves and have-nots, the demarcation between city and countryside is religiously observed in the form of ID cards and residency permits. In a heterogeneous society in the post-colonial age, the "familiar alignment of colonial subjects—Black/White, Self/Other"[6]—is a dominant motif. In a racially homogeneous society, such as China, the country/city duality takes priority. There is, however, a third space—the in-between space, the threshold, the void—that carries the burden of the meaning of culture, according to Bhabha:

The representation of difference must not be hastily read as the reflection of *pre-given* ethnic or cultural traits set in the fixed tablet of tradition. The social articulation of difference, from the minority perspective, is a complex, on-going negotiation that seeks to authorize cultural hybridities that emerge in moments of historical transformation.[7]

To document and analyze the work of the emerging farmer-writers is on the one hand an acknowledgement of the urban and rural divide and, on the other, an attempt to highlight the erosion of borders at the in-between place. "A boundary is not that at which something stops but, as the Greeks recognized, the boundary is that from which something begins its presencing."[8]
True to its core, a new "presencing" is taking place in Xi-HaiGu, ironically thanks to an erasure initiated by the Chinese government in 2011. Billed as an "ecological migration," the government plans to move more than 350,000 villagers to a manmade settlement community whose neat rows of apartments resemble Levittown on Long Island. The caravan of the

[6] Bhabha, *Location*, p. 58.

[7] *Ibid*, p. 3.

[8] Martin Heidegger, "Building, dwelling, thinking," in *Poetry, Language, Thought* (New York: Harper & Row, 1971), pp. 152–3.

first cohort, touted as part of a five-year plan, took ten hours to reach the resettlement district some thousand miles away. The drastic move has taken its toll. To fifty-year-old resident Mei Ma, XiHaiGu is the only home she knew. Married into the village at age 17, Ma couldn't help doubling back three times to the courtyard of her tamped-earth and brick house now lying in a pile of rubble. With tears running down her cheeks, Ma saw her life buried under the broken bricks and tiles that she had helped her husband lay for their modest home. Along with the abandonment and disappearance of the XiHaiGu topography comes the erasure of these writers' rootedness that has nonetheless inspired their imagination. The sadness is evident in "Village," Yue Chang-hong's (岳昌鸿)[9] homage to his birthplace:

Village
demolished and migrated as a unit
I was conspiring to destroy you
when I signed the agreement on Mother's behalf
selling out my hometown
betraying my childhood, stunting a tree's growth
spilling all the secrets inside the old house.
The old walls crumbled under the bulldozer like thin paper
uprooting my birth origin
along with old furniture, chucked out in the open
collapsing under the sun.
Chunks of the old house
cascading down unidentifiable bones.
We no longer have a home.
Hugging my father's portrait
as if Father's hugging me
over this vast empty land
no one ever will holler to beckon me home.

---

[9] Chang-hong Yue (b. 1970), a Han Chinese, serves as the chairperson of the Literary and Art Federation at Pingluo Prefecture in Ningxia. Collections of his poetry and essays have been reviewed in literary journals, where I first encountered this poem, which I translated into English because it expresses a prevalent sentiment of displacement shared by Chinese writers.

The Pastoral Mode, West and East

The division between rural and urban is hardly a new theme in literature. Theocritus (300–260 BCE), with his idealized accounts of shepherds living simple, virtuous lives in the mountainous region of Arcadia, was a pioneer of the mode:

> When Adonis o'er the sheep
> In the hills his watch did keep,
> The Love-Dame proved so wild a wooer,
> E'en in death she clips him to her.
> *Idyll III*, 2. lines 47–51

Virgil modeled his *Eclogues* on Theocritus, evoking a "golden age" in which innocent shepherds lived in primitive bliss. His bucolic poems extolled the innocent to his fellow Romans who, he feared, had strayed from civilized values. Pastoral imagery later became an important feature of Judeo-Christian doctrine, with Christ as the shepherd tending the flock, his congregation. Such traditions certainly enhanced the conviction that the shepherd's life was a paradigm of tranquility and harmonious, unconditional love as well as purity.

Theorists of the Western tradition have questioned the sincerity of such urbane pastoral writers as Virgil. In *The Oaten Flute*, the Harvard Professor of Slavic and Comparative Literature Renato Poggioli called pastoral idealism "the wishful dream of a happiness to be gained without effort, of an erotic bliss made absolute by its own irresponsibility."[10] He cautioned that the double longing after innocence and happiness is not a pure pursuit because it is not earned through suffering and sacrifice. Poggioli suggests that the bucolic ideal of moral truth beyond the strife of human contact is, at best, wishful idealism. Renouncing the city to embrace the rural as a rejection of ambition and greed is more romantic than realistic, and even hypocritical in the case of court poets (think of the cult of the pastoral at Versailles). The shepherd mitigates his pastoral "poverty"

---

[10] Renato Poggioli, *The Oaten Flute: Essays on Pastoral Poetry and the Pastoral Ideal* (Cambridge, MA: Harvard University Press, 1975), p. 14.

by enjoying the blessings of idleness. As Poggioli observes, the pastoral poet "finds his emblem not in the wise and prudent ant ...who works all year round to be ready to face the challenge of winter, but in the carefree grasshopper, who spends all summer in song and dance."[11] This recalls his neighbors criticizing Zhang Lian's writing as evidence of his lack of assiduity as a farmer.

Zhang's poems, although they follow the pastoral tradition, are different in significant ways. His understanding of rural life is real, not feigned. The unrestrained pleasures of the Renaissance pastoral would surely disqualify the pastoral as proletarian art in content or intent. Affecting a melancholy tone, the pastoral poet is simultaneously pursuing a simple, yet carefree lifestyle, lamenting his loss of innocence. In truth, however, he is less a proletarian celebrating the hardship of a poor herdsman than an actor. Even Theocritus pretended to be a shepherd, although in reality he was born and lived in advanced cities, Syracuse and Alexandria. As William Empson argues in his seminal work, *Some Versions of Pastoral*, such literature may be about the poor, but its hero is more often the sentimental bourgeois who sings songs *about* the poor but "not 'by' or 'for'" [12] them. They did not live the real pastoral life, only imagined it.

Our poet Zhang Lian is a departure. He really is a poor herdsman and farmer, and his voice is by, about, and for his people. Should we label Zhang's work proletarian? Although one might infer a political stance, I believe Zhang is more correctly viewed as an emerging literary voice for China's new era, his work an antidote to urban materialism. Its hold on modern and contemporary writers comes from a fundamental attraction to the similarly rustic ideal as the demands of society grow increasingly taxing and the sprawling urban environment is dangerously toxic in a literal sense. Our yearning for a lost innocence, for a pre-Fall paradisal life in which man existed in harmony with nature, will only grow as we careen toward a climate apocalypse.

---

[11] *Ibid*, p. 5.

[12] William Empson, *Some Versions of Pastoral: Literary Criticism* (New York: New Directions, 1974), p 6.

As in Western literature, the Chinese pastoral tradition has a long history. It dates back to the Zhou Dynasty (1027–771 BC) when the first recorded literature, the *Shi Jing* (诗经 *Book of Odes*), emerged. This seminal collection, to which later works were added, spanned the Spring and Autumn Period (770–476 BC). The first section of the *Book of Odes*, titled *Guo Feng,* or "Airs of the States," portrayed ordinary people in songs, ballads, and hymns. The pastoral tenor of these works is attested to in the way the *Book of Odes* chronicles over a hundred kinds of plants and trees, close to a hundred animal and insect species along with folkloric musical instruments, and food and clothing that are a vivid window upon early Chinese civilization, especially in the countryside. These ancient texts, though written by the literati of the court, are nonetheless focused on the common people. As with Homer's cadence and alliteration, their mnemonic rhythms and rhymes trip off the tongue smoothly and musically. With some exceptions, most lines in the *Shi Jing* comprise four characters that run three stanzas, varying in length. One favorite is the opening *si zi shijing* (four-words-per-line ballad) titled "Guan Guan Ju Jiu":

关关雎鸠	Quack, quack the bird sings
在河之洲	o'er the riverbank yonder
窈窕淑女	a lovely maiden
君子好逑	eagerly sought after
参差荇菜	Watercress high and low
左右流之	here and there plucked by many
窈窕淑女	a lovely maiden
寤寐求之	chased after day and night

The pastoral tradition in Chinese literature thrived through the ages, and in the fourth and fifth centuries, Tao Yuan-ming (陶渊明, 352–427) produced a masterful body of poetry and essays emulated later by well-known Tang poets. The pastoral reflected the longing for a remote, earthly utopia when the country was divided by constant war and political upheaval. Tao Yuan-ming's "Peach Blossom Spring" became the classic expression of nostalgia for a simpler and more peaceful life that proves illusory. Tang poets such as the renowned Li Bai (李白, 701–762), Du Fu (杜甫, 712–770), and Bai Juyi (白居易, 772–864) lived in exile from the capital, often in mountain sanctuaries where they rhapsodized over the simple wisdom that could be found in a "rural retreat." Different from Zhang Lian, these renowned masters of Chinese poetry experienced nature not as indigenous, native writers but as visitors in whose eyes the pastures, cliffs, and rivers far from the capital had an exotic allure. The lyrical power of the Tang pastoral tradition draws more on the sense of loss while seeking solace in nature. Realistic and romantic at the same time, the Tang influence is still felt in allusions in modern Chinese poetry, homage to the enduring appeal of a simple way of life to creative minds. To show how close the relationship between contemporary voices and their Tang antecedents can be, compare Zhang Lian's *Twilight* poems with the classic "Looking Out Over the Plains" (野望), by Du Fu:[13]

清秋望不极	Clear autumn, sight has no bounds;
迢递起曾阴	High in the distance piling shadows rise.
远水兼天净	The farthest waters merge in the sky unsullied;
孤城隐雾深	A neglected town hides deep in mist.
叶稀风更落	Sparse leaves, which the wind still sheds,
山迥日初沈	Far hills, where the sun sinks down.
独鹤归何晚	How late the solitary crane returns!
昏鸦已满林	But the twilight crows already fill the forest.

Just as the Tang recluses whose literary landscapes, like misty ink paintings, often hid subtly acerbic critiques of urban power, contemporary Chinese pastoral poets use the genre to deliver satire. We need to remember, however, that Zhang never traveled as far and wide as those itinerant poets of the Tang Dynasty.

It is probably no coincidence that more and more Chinese writers are returning to the pastoral tradition as they witness the worrisome toll of vast economic growth, depletion of resources, and contamination of nature's most precious gifts: water and

---

[13] "Looking Out Over the Plains," tranlsated by Graham, A.C., *Anthology of Chinese Literature,* Cyril Birch, ed. (New York: Grove Press, 1965) p. 238.

air. The parallels are striking. As in today's China, during the relatively peaceful Tang dynasty the country experienced roaring economic growth that led to the opulent lifestyle at the emperor's palace and and among a growing class of wealthy citizens. China's literati today are turning their attention to the emerging pastoral writers, such as Zhang, for a renewed sense of meaning. Readers can trust the sincerity of his depiction of rural reality from first-hand experience, an honest life etched in the lines of daily poems that exude peace and hope.

Translating Zhang Lian

For this volume, I selected one hundred poems from over three-thousand composed by Zhang in his time spared from farming duties. They chiefly represent his multifaceted perceptions of his world at dusk, the only free time in a day's hard labor, when the shepherd is blessed with a moment to daydream. Facing the "same" twilight each day, Zhang Lian saw different colors, images, and prospects, whose impressions he harnessed as material. With only the natural scenery Zhang Lian could afford to experience daily, the poet produced a collection of images that are vastly diverse. He observed:

> My poetry, every poem, is a picture, a conception, a fairy tale, a story. They record the path I trek, the scenery I see each day, my feelings and emotions at the time, and man's struggle to battle hardship and achieve happiness; to ponder life, vitality, nature, and the environment. They represent quietude, solitude, and deep thoughts; nature is the entry point of a solitary poet: his extreme quietude, deep solitude, and profound reflection.

Zhang Lian uses the local vernacular to invoke a tranquil, contented lifestyle in a rural setting of light and color, through which a magnificent twilight unfailingly guides farmers and shepherds homeward. Although the land may no longer be theirs, through his poetry Zhang stubbornly keeps both light and landscape intact and present. He makes readers feel that he is not the agent but a passive recipient of a natural beauty that allows residents to feel safe and secure.

I have attempted to reproduce verse-renderings of this vision of rural life. In selecting poems for translation, I listened to their musical qualities and searched for English equivalents not just for the rich imagery of twilight and country living as experienced through the poet's eye, but the voice of the poet for the reader's ear. Zhang Lian has an admirable knack for using silence and metrical tempo in counterpoint as the basis of his unique musical style. Consider the gentle adagio of the lines "low, dark clouds, moist village/silently the green pasture rustled" (p. 122). Monosyllables and vowels help us feel the rhythmic swaying of the grass blades, a sound that naturally drifts in the air. In "Grandson, picking up green dates/chewing in his mouth, soundless" (p. 78), Zhang challenges his reader's empathy to recognize the verisimilitude of a child eating fresh dates in an automatic torpor. The stately cadence of "a speck of twilight/by the tail of each bright day" (p. 81) slows our attention as we watch the splendid sun slowly drop below the horizon.

Zhang's poems are neither traditionally formal nor downright folkloric. Each consists of fourteen lines with occasional rhymes, but without a Shakespearean or Petrarchan sonnet rhyme scheme. In addition to the dialectal vernacular, his lines are laced with allusions to canonic classical Chinese poetry. For example, in modern Chinese *putonghua* (common language), the informal expression for an idle person, "one with no work to do," (没有事做的人) becomes "idler" (闲) a more formal expression used for a poetic effect. According to the poet, the word "idler" throughout his poetry collection refers to himself, reflecting what the villagers consider him. Zhang also coined "formal" expressions that are vernacular-based, such as "little people" (小人) instead of "children" (孩子), "youngsters" (后生, literally "later born") instead of "young people" (年轻人).

Allusions to Tang and Song poetry also appear in the form of borrowed words transplanted in a new context. For example, a line from the well-known Tang poet, He Zhizhang (贺知章, 695–744), reads "Spring wind of the second lunar month cuts like a pair of scissors" (二月春风似剪刀), which inspired an image in Zhang Lian's work, "A ray of twilight cuts through the doorway" (院门口裁下了一缕暮色). Here Zhang replaces the noun *jian* (剪, scissors) in the Tang poem with a verb *cai* (裁, to cut). This switch of noun to verb shows Zhang's careful adaptation of ancient diction to accommodate his compositional needs, as well as his mastery of the language, since both words are often used as a set phrase, *cai jian* (to crop).

Another example is found in "When all at once lifting my head, I notice / your extraordinary shadow" (猛然抬首却注目到). This line alludes to one from a famed Tang poem by Li Bai, "Raising my head I see the bright moon" (举头望明月), to invoke a sense of longing for home. Zhang Lian coined the expression 抬首 (*tai shou*), combining the common vernacular *tai* in *tai-tou* (lifting or raising the head) and the classical, formal *shou* (首, head) found in a Song poem by Xin Qiji (辛弃疾, 1140–1207), "When all at once I turn my head" (暮然回首). By this deft linguistic maneuver, Zhang conjures two emotions at one stroke: that of homesickness as expressed in Li Bai's classic poem and a plangent sense of displacement articulated by Xin Qiji.

On the other hand, the strict rhyme schemes integral to classical Chinese verse are nowhere to be found. When asked whether he thought about rhyme as he composed, Zhang Lian replied: "When I compose, I do not think about rhyme schemes, nor do I follow traditional Chinese poetic forms. I follow my instinctive feelings at the time and grapple with diction and word choice. There are traces of our Chinese literary tradition, but I mainly go for a musical rhythm."

Although Zhang Lian is a nature poet, his incisive imagery has rich social and philosophical undertones. In "The Cellar" (p. 45) Zhang subtly alludes to the 1950s famine caused by Mao's ideological movement known as the Great Leap Forward: "my sweat pickled skin must be very delicious / used for a drum it must also be extremely resonant" (被汗水淹得很熟的皮肤一定很香 / 如果能做一面鼓也一定很响). The two lines daringly invoke the unofficial accounts of cannibalism during the famine in the 1950s while the country celebrated Mao's vision daily with propaganda drum troupes on the street. Zhang's ability to pursue artistic beauty amid abject poverty attests to the resilience of the creative mind. Harsh reality lends strength to his voice and pushes him to philosophize.

Zhang Lian's poems appear here in English translation for the first time. The project's importance partly lies in the poignant realization that the place that gave birth to such imaginative and powerful poetry is about to disappear, obliterated by the central government's massive infrastructure plans. Birthplace "predisposes one to retain quaint ideas about matter and thought," notes Allan Sekula.[14] Soon such "matter and thought" will vanish along with the topography of Ningxia as part of the government's strategic intervention. Zhang Lian's *Twilight* captures both hopefulness and hopelessness, and a deep belief in the redemptive power of words. "My poetry is the voice of solitude, loneliness, and privacy; it is not intended to fit in or to be fashionable," the poet asserts. "Twilight is a super space, a mother figure, a spiritual reality that affords me motherly love and care." To Zhang, the countryside is the land of poetry.

[14] Allan Sekula, *Fish Story* (Düsseldorf, Germany: Richter Verlag, 1995), p. 12.

TWILIGHT
傍晚

那里有一片落霞

你一定知道
三十九号桩处
那里有一片落霞
你曾
为了走进那片绚烂
一定会走去
沿着通过你村子的公路
向村外走去
那就是傍晚
三十九号桩处
那片好大好大的碱水湖旁
紫红紫红的一朵朵
组成的一片的
傍晚

A Patch of Falling Color

You must be aware
over in Village 39
there is a patch of falling color.
You were once bent
on entering that patch of splendor
determined to follow
the highway, through your village
and out, leaving it behind
in the twilight.
In Village 39
by a large alkaline lake
tufts and tufts of purple
form a patch of
twilight.

取水在暮色里

取水在暮色里
窖中取水倒进厨房缸中
在这样的春日寂静里，我忙于经营
经营一种感情经营钱的变换让钱变成物
又让钱从物中变了回来
让我花言巧语 用尽心机
面对芸芸众生 经营我的感情
让人们买去 买去吧 那是钱的虚身
在那虚身里 那是你们生活的需要吗
让我在生命街能站多久 就站多久
看那西天里的霞色 暗的深沉
在赭黄赭红里 衬着极兰的净空
鸦儿又从头顶飞过去
归去吧 带去小村的宁静

Fetching Water in Twilight

Gathering water in twilight
pouring well water into the kitchen jar.
In such quiet moments I busy myself
trading emotions, converting money into things
then turning things back into money.
Exhausted with my sweet words
I transact my emotions with the crowd:
"Go, go shopping! Test your money's face value.
Is your life fulfilled by that purchased reality?"
Allow me to stand at the intersection of life, however long
watching the western sky's glow subside.
The indigo sky dipped in orange red
disturbed only by birds,
carrying the village peace away over my head.

淡淡的紫色

淡淡的紫色在西天里
连着天际
淡淡的蓝色在天空里
连着紫色
淡淡的黄色在天空上
连着小村
似一束鸟的羽翼
淡淡的一弯白色在高空上
连着西天
变幻着的是那鸟的羽翼
在绯红里
似一归巢的鸦鸣
几个驼着背的人正走进村去
经过几株炭黑的树身

A Touch of Purple

Lilac suffuses the Western sky
connected with the horizon.
Powder blue ascends, its edge
touching the purple border.
A band of lemon-yellow floats above them
leading to the village,
colors arrayed like a flock of geese on the wing.
A sliver of white
appears in the sky, the crescent moon on the rise.
The only movement is the beat of the wings of the birds
in the incandescent red
honking to signal the arrival of autumn.
A few hunchbacks saunter toward the village
threading their paths through grayish-black trunks of the
　　　forest.

世界原来在这里落幕

我的煤车已驰过
你的村子
一个傍晚
太阳正红的浑圆
正在靠近这片绚烂
亮的湖
红的霞
我透过你榆林稀疏的村旁
想起你
为了这片绚烂
我在想　你一定也会走去
迎着此时的神洁辉煌
世界的傍晚原来就在这里落幕
我的心不愿离去

The World Pulls Down Its Curtain Here

My coal truck passed by your village
one evening.
When the sun burned red
mounting a patch of gorgeous splendor.
Glowing lake
cloud ablaze
passing through the patchy elm trees
I think of you again.
For this patch of glorious color,
you must be heading out, I conjecture,
to embrace the magical light.
The world's dusk
pulls down its curtain here
and my heart is reluctant to depart.

窑

傍晚走出窑　才知东西[1]

怎知白日里打着窑进入土里

被汗水淹着皮肤

此时整个身躯

如一粒沸水后的熟米

在日暮里看暮色消沉

低首看窑内一片空茫

我在想

被汗水淹得很熟的皮肤一定很香[2]

如果能做一面鼓也一定很响

我在想

在窑底里深处思想

看天的出口处

才知窑原本是天地下一个最大的容器.[3]

[1] 为了配合英文语法规范，译者在英译文内加入代名词"我"。中文文法在此不需"我"这个代名词，但读者可以自然理解诗内人物的语言对象。

[2] 中文里"香"(xiāng)和"响"(xiǎng)是同音词。"香"为平声，"响"为去声。从诗的韵律角度来说，"香"和"响"押韵。香甜可口，淹制得当的皮肤吃起来一定很香是一句当今不可思议的。但在50年代的中国大跃进时期，由于自然和人为的灾害，大面积土地没有收成，贫苦的农民在重压下出现人吃人的现象。这一历史见证在Jason Becker 1997 年所著的《死鬼：毛的秘密饥荒》被描述的淋漓尽致。据统计，三千多万人口死于饥荒。

[3] 此篇诗歌引用中国成语"井底之蛙"，也称"坐井观天"，比喻眼光狭隘　且自以为是的愚昧之人　这首诗引用中国一句成语"井底之蛙"来描述目光狭窄，自以为是的小人，坐在井底看到井口的一片天，便以为这就是世界所有的天地了。

44

Root Cellar

Emerging from the cellar after dusk, I discover East and West.[1]
It turned out I had entered Earth while digging the cellar;
my skin is pickled in my sweat,
and my body
as if a cooked kernel of grain in boiling water.
Watching the disappearance of twilight
lowering my head to witness the emptiness in the cellar
I ponder:
my sweat-pickled skin must be very delicious.[2]
Used for a drum, it must also be extremely resonant;
I contemplate
thoughts at the bottom of the cellar.
Looking up at sky's exit
I realize that my cellar is the largest container under heaven.[3]

[1] In the Chinese text the poet does not identify himself with the pronoun "I" until the eighth line, which is repeated in line 11. Given the structure and syntax of Chinese, the identity of the speaker is obvious, although the English translation would sound awkward without a pronoun. Thus here and elsewhere pronouns are added where necessary. As well, in English verse punctuation and capitalization are typically used to clarify textual flow. Chinese orthography, on the other hand, lacks capitals, and Chinese poetry (and prose) traditionally lacked punctuation.

[2] The characters xiāng (香, meaning fragrant, delicious) and xiǎng (响, meaning loud) which end the lines, are homophones, emphasizing the poet's musings on the various uses of human skin. "Delicious pickled human skin" evokes cannibalism reportedly practiced during the 1950s famine caused by Mao's Great Leap Forward. In *Hungry Ghosts: Mao's Secret Famine* (NY: The Free Press, 1997), Jasper Becker reports that over thirty million people starved to death. This line is a subtle stab at the misguided policies that contributed to the dire poverty that persists in some areas of rural China to this day.

[3] This poem alludes to a well-known Chinese expression, "the frog at the bottom of the well" (井底之蛙), which describes the narrow-minded view of a self-righteous yet ignorant person whose vision is confined to a limited patch of sky seen from the bottom of a well, but taken as the whole universe.

驼着背的人[4]

天底下
几个驼着背的人
正走进村去
在淡淡的青色里
村间走动
青色的天空
青色的暮色
青色的树桠
青色的人
青色的房
舍旁一株树桠里
一抹淡红移动
移动着宁静
移动着几个驼背的人

[4] 诗人张联在微信箱回答我提出的问题时说:《傍晚集》第54页: "几个驼着背的人": 这个意象的产生是来自现实场景, 夕阳西下时的劳动者的身影, 从村外的原野里回来, 驼着背, 背负着一天中采挖后的药材, 正在归来。寓意: 如法国著名作家波德莱尔的名篇《每个人的怪兽》, 因为人类总是在一种不可控制的行走欲中推动着, 不停地向前的进程。2016.10.10早晨盐池. 张联羡慕这些无人闻知, 无人揭晓的农民们, 他们在如此艰难困苦的土地上, 依然保存着永久希望下去的精神。他们不图名誉, 不抱任何幻想, 只是安安稳稳地耕田, 务农, 生活, 生育, 为炎黄子孙贡献自己微薄的所有.

The Hunchbacks[4]

Under heaven

a few hunchbacks

are entering the village.

In the gentle touch of dark blue

the village is moving;

the dark blue sky

the dark blue twilight

the dark blue tree branches

the dark blue people

the dark blue houses.

In the tree branches by a house

a touch of red, moving

carrying with it peacefulness

and a few hunchbacked men.

[4] See p. 20 for the influence of Charles Baudelaire's "Chacun sa Chimère" ("To Each His Own Chimera") on the creation of this poem.

我提着我的皮走动在大街上[5]

我提着我的皮走动在大街上

我在这富有的人群中走动身无分文

走进繁华的商场

我提着我的皮走动却无力张望这个世界

我在这富有的人群中走动

带着一颗干瘪的心

我不能停下来张望或者歇一歇

只因我没有脚凳也就无处歇足

我提着我的皮走动

无心廉价地出售自己的灵魂

可是啊一辆车内塞满了富有的微笑

塞满了华丽的服饰和年货的拥挤

在今天世界上挤扁了一个灵魂

我又能逃向哪里？即使是一粒尘埃也要落地。

[5] 在2000和2001年间，干旱造成大幅度干旱，张联为了给孩子们提供一个丰盛的新年年夜饭，准备一些传统的新年零食，除夕那天他步行20多公里，带着家里唯一有点价值的羊皮，到集市来卖。一天过去后，羊皮还没卖掉，张联内心充满懊丧，拖着沉重的脚步，在回家的路上写下这首感人的诗篇。

I Trudge with my Skin in My Hand[5]

I trudge with my skin in my hand
among the rich crowd, owning not a penny
entering the cacophonous market.
I plod with my skin in my hand, no energy to take in the world
among the rich crowd,
dragging a crushed heart.
I cannot stop to explore, or to take a rest.
I own not a stool, no place to put up my feet.
I slog with my skin in my hand
no desire to sell out my soul.
But a truck loaded with smile
crowded to the brim with beautiful clothes and New Year's
    goods!
A soul is crushed flat today.
To where can I flee? Even a speck of dust has to return to the
    ground.

[5] The dramatic circumstances surrounding this first major poem written by Zhang Lian are described in detail on p. 16.

一唇天

淡淡的云　悠悠的风　薄薄的暮色

我在西天锄葵　离村三四里

暮归的羊儿移动着　一片声响

不觉回眸　羊儿已远去[6]

静在空旷里响

天际里有一唇天　泛红

我和妻归去　走过油菜地

惊起白蝶黄花飞

走在草场里　牧草婆莎摇摆[7]

东天里满月儿正白

淡淡的云儿　正渐渐微红

人到院落里　忙于晚炊

小儿在等待里打盹

静在院中响

---

[6] 此行引用宋代诗人辛弃疾 (1140-1207) 的著名诗作,《青玉案•元夕》,张联更换原词中 "暮然回首" 一句为 "不觉回眸。" 用自然生活中常用语 "不觉" 取代文言正式词语 "暮然"；用修辞中的换喻手法以乡间土语 "眸"（眼睛的意思）来代替 "首"（头部）。

[7] "唇" 自然把读者的注意力集中到女子红唇之象征。诗人在此并不直接描述男人对女人的渴望之欲,但用婉转的手法描述小脚女人窈窕淑女般行走的意向,以间接手法道出乡村男人的欲念。当然,此欲念不仅局限于乡间男人,但他们农田里不可能接触到那些电视上看到的城市小姐们,他们的女人是粗手大脚在地里耕劳的女人。

A Lip of Sky

Faint cloud, leisurely wind, thin twilight
I harvest sunflowers, a mile or more from home.
My sheep gambol home in twilight, creating a field of sound
when all at once turning my gaze, I see my sheep already in
    the distance[6]
silence rings in the open.
A lip of sky forms on the horizon, a patch of red.
My wife and I pass by a mustard field
stirring a host of white moths, pollen flies.
Over the field, tall weeds sway dancing[7]
the wintry moon brightly shining
faint cloud turning pinkish red
people busy with outdoor cooking
children dozing while waiting
and silence rings in the yard.

---

[6] This line alludes to a famous Song dynasty poem by Xin Qiji (1140–1207), "To the Tune of A Green Jadeite Plate," written on the first day of the Gregorian calendar. Zhang Lian uses the same sequence of the four-word line in the original Chinese, *mu-ran hui-shou* (All of a sudden turning my head) but applies a new expression, *bu-jue hui-mu* (When all at once turning my gaze), replacing *mu-ran* (suddenly). The latter is an example of high literary diction drawing on the Chinese classics, while *bu-jue* (with little notice or suddenly) is a common example of vernacular expression. The original *shou* (head) is replaced by *mu* (eyes), a clever application of synecdoche.

[7] The poet subtly suggests, invoking an ancient aesthetic of feminine beauty, the farmer's desire for a traditional lady with enticing bound feet, sashaying around unlike the woman next to him in the field. Yet, he cannot afford such luxury on the farm. It is left to the reader's imagination to comprehend the farmer's longings and his helplessness at being a poor farmer while watching the young ladies in high heels on sophisticated TV shows.

鲜唇

漫天阴云　在七月八日里
使牧羊人迷失了方向
驱赶着羊儿向村里逃
逃至村旁
须间　天地里豁然暴亮
回首里
一抹浓烟的鲜唇
在村旁里
正滑落着时间
直到浑圆
羊儿惊叫里
怎知暮色正红
飘逸了的晚霞
在苍穹的阴云里

Bright Lips

Dark clouds fill the sky on July eighth
causing the shepherd to lose his way
herding his sheep toward the village
at the edge of town.
Suddenly, the sky breaks open
looking back
a stroke of gaudy lips
at the edge of town
chisels away the hour
to a rounded ball.
Amid the loud bleating
dusk turns into its brightest red
elegance of the sunset
inside the heavy clouds of the sky.

黄门帘[8]

冬的
农历十月中旬的一个傍晚
太阳是一个暖暖的黄门帘
低低地垂挂着
映照着一户土墙屋的门面
一个黄色的门帘
门帘旁有两个黄色的小丫丫
正依着土屋
黄色的墙面
不知分吃着土屋里悄拿的什么东西
在黄的暖暖的宁静里依着
一个黄色的门帘
在冬的傍晚的一个门前
低低垂挂着的黄门帘

Yellow Door Curtain[8]

It was winter,
a mid-October evening in the Lunar calendar
the sun formed a warm yellow door curtain
hanging low
reflected on a clay hovel's doorway
a yellow door curtain.
Two little girls stood by the curtain
nestled into the clay shack
against its yellow walls
sharing God-knows-what snacks quietly taken from within.
Leaning against the yellow warm serenity
was a yellow door curtain
over the door of a winter twilight
a low-hanging yellow door curtain.

8 译者用微信提问诗人张联 "黄" 的内在含义，诗人回信说："一个暖暖的黄门帘："特指那时傍晚的太阳，是那么强烈而神性地挂在西天上，临照着现实中的一个黄色的小门帘。如此之近，也如此之温馨，或上帝，此刻的博爱更加让贫瘠土地上居住的村庄和人性更加的温暖。也就是说，人类在生存的生命史过程中，心灵和灵魂能够得到更大的拯救。是来于大自然。

8 Zhang Lian explains the significance of yellow in several of his poems: "It refers to evening sun—so intense, so divine, hanging in the sky, casting its rich color over the curtain on the door. It is so close, so comforting, like God offering love to the poor people in the poverty-stricken region on the steppe. In other words, man's existence, heart or soul, receives salvation from nature."

一轮黄月亮[9]

日落村间后

寂静幽长

醒着的两面墙

相对着

一个醒着的场

闲人走过来

提着一袋暮色和牲口

一串足音在响

墙头上擎着一轮黄月亮

和几面树冠清幽幽的寂长

在淡蓝的天空下

闲人走过来[10]

寂静幽长

醒着的两面墙和一个场

[9] 墙头上擎着一轮黄月亮: "这一意象的象征，在我的心中应该是神的又一次来临。在我眼中看到暮色中村庄的宁静，神秘和美好，是来自这一黄月亮的恩赐。而我更像一个天地间的清醒者一样，能够超越常人，是唯一一个在场的旁观者和亲临者，来完成这一神圣母爱来临的过程。可以说，我的所有诗作，都是在这一旁观者和亲临者的状态中完成（8:15 PM 盐池。2016年10月1日早晨）请参考上首诗《黄门帘》注解.

[10] "闲人"在所有诗作里都是指作者张联，诗人自己。这个词是地方语，意思是没有事可做的人。诗中闲人是诗人自谦：这样一个没有能力做好其他事情，而只会写诗的人.

Yellow Moon[9]

The village after the sunset

drifts into a stretch of quiet

two wide-awake walls

facing each other.

In a vigilant square

idlers saunter

with a bag of twilight and a donkey,

a bell punctuating its steps.

The walls hold a crescent of yellow moon

and a canopy of silence over treetops.

Under the powder-blue sky

idlers come.[10]

The silence is long

with two wide-awake walls and a watchful square.

[9] Zhang Lian confesses that the yellow moon at twilight evokes in him a mysterious feeling of solitude when he is both a bystander watching the magnificent light and a participant immersed in the transient silence and heavenly color. See also note 8 on the significance of yellow to the poet.

[10] The poet has explained that "idler" is a self-deprecatory reference to his own reputation in the village, where his hard-working neighbors consider him a dilettante rather than a dedicated shepherd and farmer. It uses a colloquial expression to describe a person who dilly dallies all day long. Its literary origin can be traced to the Belle Epoque Parisian tradition of the *flaneur*, which Charles Baudelaire (a favorite of Zhang Lian) used to describe himself.

夏的五月[11]

傍晚里

我在这夏的五月的院门口　徘徊

看西天里落日正红

青的云霞在天际

有几条艳的霞带

两小儿

在西天下的门口玩泥

正捏造一个泥人

谁知这髦年玩童

在嬉笑里借落日的霞迹

我想着炉台正煮着米

看那老屋的院角处

那夏的灰色浓发

正纷飞着划向天际

---

[11] 按照农历/阴历日历，月份和四季都比阳历日历上晚一个月或者一个多月，那要根据每个年头的闰年是几天。"在这个夏的五月"中的"五月"在阳历日历上则是六月份，夏初时节了。阴历日历按照月亮周转计算月份，阴历月份都是20天至30天内，导致阴历月份一般比阳历月份晚到21天至51天。

Summer's May[11]

At dusk
I linger at the gate of early summer
contemplating the red setting sun in the western sky
dark clouds on the horizon
crisscrossing strips of color.
Two children
kneading clay under the western sky
modeling a clay man.
Oh the tender-aged children
laughing and playing under the sunset.
I remember my rice is cooking on the stove
in the corner of the old courtyard
the summer's grey thick mane
gliding through the sky.

[11] Months and seasons begin later using the lunar calendar. This "summer's May" would
be June in the Gregorian calendar.

时间的伤口

十一月二十五日
坐在班车上
面对冬日的西南山上
在这样一个流动的窗口里
落日在低空里飞行
一个圆的橙色里　宁静的余辉
洁然地满布山野
这样的窗口里　有几缕流动的光
正在一个少女侧着的面颊上流动
这样一个冬日里
温暖如春　暮色苍茫
正在西南的山下
看落日滑行时擦伤着
一个时间的伤口

The Wounds of Time

November twenty-fifth
on board a bus
facing winter's southwest mountains
through such a moving window
the setting sun flies low.
Within a round orange, calm remains of the day
cascade smoothly over the mountains.
Through the window are a few strands of light
floating, down on a girl's cheek.
On such a wintry day
warm as spring, boundless twilight
at the foot of the southwestern mountains
watching the setting sun sliding, scraping
the wounds of time.

暮的巢穴

昨日里
银样的彩霞飞逸着
向东天里移动
渐渐暗淡
在淡青色里沉寂
落日在淡白淡黄里
渐渐沉寂
西天里有浊的青气
一只红色的小鸟
还在院门口的草丝里
追逐暮色里的飞虫
那是很微小的一对亮的翅膀
正飞翔着
投递一个暮的巢穴

A Twilight Nest

Yesterday
silvery, colorful clouds fly
toward the eastern sky
gradually getting dark
submerging into a dark blue, into silence;
the sun setting into pale yellow
gradually, silently.
Over the western sky hovers a turbid haze
a red bird
in the grass by the courtyard gate
chasing a moth in twilight
with its tiny pair of bright wings
fluttering
delivering a twilight nest.

有一个名字叫簇拥

这样的傍晚
羊群簇拥着我山峦簇拥着我草地簇拥着我
我便认为有一个名字叫簇拥
这样的傍晚
落日簇拥着我月儿簇拥着我蛾儿簇拥着我
一切簇拥的簇拥着我
我在窒息中吮吸着簇拥的馨香
我便认为有一个名字叫簇拥
我看着窒息氛围外的天空
只见无数眨着眼睛的下来
这样的傍晚我逃进了我的斗室
顿觉一片空落落的声响
只因室内没有妻的簇拥
夜已坐在我的窗台上沐浴月光

A Name Called Embracing

On such an evening
my sheep nestle into me, mountains surround me, and the
    prairie envelops me.
I am made to believe there's a name called *embracing*.
On such an evening
the sun sets on me, the moon creeps up over me, moths
    encircle me
all revolving around me.
I inhale the enveloping fragrance, choking
convinced that there's a name called *embracing*.
Peeping through the suffocating thickness, the sky
falls in countless shards of light.
I tuck into my sheepfold
feeling the spread of hollow noises.
In the absence of my wife's embrace
night settles on the moonlit windowsill.

蹲伏在村外的情绪[12]

夏日的傍晚西天里
层层的云层变成了血红
村子里的
几棵炭黑的树身
飞上了彩霞
暮色正悄悄地从树身下来
走进芊芊草丛
驱赶着我的羊儿要拥抱栅栏
层层的云层变成了血红
苍穹的无数蓝色
正飞速般
流向苍白的一枚弯月
西天里紫红紫红
只剩下人儿蹲伏在村外的情绪

Crouching Sentiment[12]

The summer sun sits in the western sky
dying the clouds bloody red.
Inside the village
a few darkened tree trunks
daubed with color
down which slide shadows of dusk
sinking into the soft tufts of grass.
Herding my sheep, I wish to hug a fence
layers of clouds dripping red.
Heaven's numerous blues
sent into flight
toward the sickle of the moon
the crimson western sky
leaving the shepherd crouching, at the village end.

¹² 张联说 "这首诗是我初期状态（1993年7月26日初夜写成）：从学生时期回到农耕时代中，
对小村和大自然的一次真正的融入。或是心灵安放在母体中的一次思想的清晰呈现，可以说
时光在前进着，暮色来临到夜色笼罩，世界那一刻只剩下我一个醒着的蹲伏，和一个诗人在
我心里的出现和诞生。"蹲伏"这是两个动作的完成。"蹲"是让夜色的天空更高，也是让
身体更靠近大地，是有一种心里温暖的感觉，交给个夜交给了村子。"伏"是向前或向下，
更靠近一些的，心里作用下的，得到大地的拥抱。"

¹² Zhang Lian explained that this poem was composed during the early stages of his life
as a writer (on July 26, 1993, he was 26). After graduating from high school and working
as a part-time teacher in an elementary school, Zhang returned to his home village where
he started the life of a farmer and herder. "It was my first encounter with nature in an
extremely intimate way. I felt that for the first time I was thinking on my own, feeling
the march of time, a kind of coming-of-age epiphany. I was alone in the world at that
moment and the poet that I was to become started to emerge inside my heart as if I were
reborn. 'Crouching' refers to the squatting position assumed with a leaning upper body.
To 'crouch' is to make the night sky appear even higher while also pushing my body closer
to the earth, a sort of psychological warmth generated when in touch with nature, aban-
doning myself to the night, to the village. 'Leaning' makes that connection even tighter."

在太阳落下山的一刻中

在太阳落下山的一刻中
我注目着西天里的那些云彩
铅灰色已被农家房舍的土色遮去了许多
这时还没到需要拉亮户内灯光的时候
一弯淡淡的月牙儿光正在增着亮
两条平行线正在村落间的上空
飞速地串着恬静
就在那空中挑着暮色加深时
我的确要去柴堆旁
拿一把放的很干的老瓜头
此时
村落间已无人走动也没有狗的身影
当我的情绪从坑的烟囱里冒着火星
便是暮色沉沉了

The Sunset Moment

At the moment of the setting sun
I stare at the iridescent western sky.
The peasants' huts shrouded by the pewter clouds
still not time to turn on the light.
Under the crescent moon
are two parallel lines
over the horizon, spearing the quiet
of a darkening sky.
I must go to the haystack
to collect a bundle of dry kindling.
At this moment
no souls stirring, no dogs barking
when my mood is about to ignite
it's already late in the day.

这样的两个黑色的精灵

屋檐下的两只燕子
这样的两个黑色的精灵
正叽咕地对话在白色的线上
来了多久呢今日我才留意
不知何时才用香甜的枝蔓
构筑我久居的巢
妻在院中也学着叽咕声哄两个孩子玩
不吃红谷子不吃绿糜子借你家的屋檐抱儿子
谁知另一边院里的三只鸡
在白色的院面上擦洗着喙
然后啄着周身沐浴
并无意回到窝里
两个黑色的精灵在暗淡的光里
叽咕成暮色

Two Black Spirits

Under the eave two barn swallows—
these two black spirits
perch on the white beam chattering.
I only noticed them today.
Since when did they build their nest
using my hay to fortify our hut?
Muttering like birds, my wife plays with the kids:
"No sorghum, no beans, borrow your hut to produce a son."
Three roosters pecking in the yard
preening against the white yard
fluttering and pecking while bathing
no intention of returning to their coop.
Two black swallows in the darkening light
chattering into dusk.

滑落那颗杏树上的几声啁啾

你看这户内户外
在傍晚里
为了晚餐
小鸡在叫小猪在叫孩子在叫
叫声里有妻的牢骚
为了屋檐下的霞光和宁静
燕子在叫
我只好
在院门前的草坪上
听白色的小羊在叫
凉爽的西风吹来
毛玻璃似的太阳
正在村旁
滑落那颗杏树上的几声啁啾

Chirping over the Apricot Tree

Inside and outside
near dark
for supper
chicks chirping, pigs oinking, a child crying.
Joining the cacophony, wife's complaint.
For the quietude under the eave
I focus on the bird's cry;
Craning my neck
to catch the white-fleeced sheep's bleating.
Over the prairie
cool breeze brushes my face
fuzzy sunlight
at the edge of town
falling past the chirping over the apricot tree.

暮色在赤黄黄的土墙壁上

傍晚的牧羊人正背对落日
看着自己的影子
坐在茂盛的草丛中
身旁的羊铃叮当
呼吸身上
一天来
太阳的焦味好香
思索着迎面风的凉意
背对落日
看着自己的影子
草丛里叮当
耳梢里的一丝灼热
羊儿已走远
暮色在赤黄黄的土墙壁上 已经很低

Twilight over the Yellow Wall

Back to the setting sun, the shepherd
contemplates his shadow
sitting in the vibrant grass
surrounded by ding-dong of bells.
Inhaling
the day
the tasty burning sun
the cool breeze on his face
back to the sunset
staring at his own shadow
ding-dong, ding-dong
a rush of heat on his ear drum
his herd drifts afar.
Dusk falls low on the yellow wall.

这阵气色很好

经过一天的闷热和浮躁
封闭了一天的户内闲人
走到户外看看天看看地
不由叹道这阵气色很好
天空里退着变化的青云
扑面刮来的是一阵阵凉爽的风
房舍旁青青草点缀着星罗棋布的暮归羊群
一轮橙色的圆太阳正徐徐落下
女人在院子里拣着韭菜
这阵气色很好
这阵气色很好
不觉暮色已隐匿了五月桃的花瓣
晚饭就要开了
我迟迟合上手中的诗集

Momentary Splendor

After a day's heat and restlessness,
after a day's cabin fever
out streams the idler
with an involuntary sigh of relief.
The sky retreats with changing clouds
a cool breeze caresses his face
the herds scatter like stars across the grass.
An orange sun slowly lowers its torso
a woman in the yard picking vegetables.
This moment is splendid
a brief splendor.
Not realizing twilight has brushed over May's peach blossoms
and suppertime overdue
I reluctantly close my poetry volume.

这个世界没有了声音

没有声音
村落里没有声音
老屋里的枣儿结着没有声音
在风中掉下来没有声音
母亲走动着没有声音
孩子拾起绿色的枣儿
吃到嘴里没有声音
整个村子没有声音
空气里迟钝的光儿没有声音
我走动着没有声音　没有声音
我说我的思维里没有声音
整个村外里没有声音
庞大的穹窿没有声音
谁在延伸着延伸着　没有声音

A Silent Realm

There is no sound.
Silence wraps the village.
The date stalks inside the old hovel release no sound.
Silence falls with the wind.
Mom's steps produce no sound.
Grandson, picking up green dates,
chewing in his mouth, soundless.
The whole village is soundless.
Dull light in the atmosphere emits no sound.
My walk produces no sound, no sound.
I say silence exists in my thinking.
Silence encircles the village.
The giant sky falls into silence,
stretching, stretching, in silence.

白日的尾里

在每个白日的尾里
一个乡间闲人
在中天里
看西天下
傍晚走来
春夏秋冬在每个白日的尾里
从落日的淡泊浑圆处
伴着不同的暗淡寂静的光彩
在宁静闲适的村街上
消融
消融在无尽的虚空里
成为
一粒暮色
在每个白日的尾里

By the Tail of Each Bright Day

By the tail of each bright day
a village idler
inside the celestial sphere
watches the underside of the western sky
where nightfall approaches.
Spring, summer, autumn, winter, by the tail of every bright day
from the thin round falling sun
with various, dim, silent, brilliant lights
on the peaceful idle country road
dissolving
disappearing into the vast void
becoming
a speck of twilight
by the tail of each bright day.

盔甲里锁着的天

天空在云的盔甲里锁着
日落时却锁不住太阳
今天他没有光彩
无色地从盔甲里出来
又走进另一个盔甲里
隐没于山那边
我和女人正背向着你走动
到村口
肩头扛着疲惫的锄
在你的意境里
猛然抬首却注目到
东天里村子的上空
确有你那非凡的身影
在那绯黄的流彩里走动

A Captive Sky

The sky is locked in a cloud helmet
that cannot contain the setting sun.
He's lackluster today,
crawling out from inside the helmet,
then entering another helmet
hiding over the mountainside.
My wife and I walk, with our backs to you
reaching the village gate
tired hoes over our shoulders.
In your sublime atmosphere,
when all at once, lifting my head, I notice
over the village's eastern sky
your extraordinary double
in that deep reddish yellow, moving.

我是谁?

我向西天奔去

大声哭泣

天是我的父亲

地是我的母亲

我为何而生　我是谁

我向西天里奔去

追逐这冬日里的淡淡霞光

大声哭泣　我是谁

天是我的父亲

地是我的母亲

我为何而生　暮色降临

在天和地的切口处

我是谁　我是谁呀

万物寂静

Who Am I?

I rush to the western sky
crying aloud:
"Sky is my father
Earth my mum."
Why was I born, and who am I?
I hasten toward the western sky
chasing winter's faint rays of light.
Crying aloud, who am I?
Sky my father
Earth mother.
For what was I born? Twilight descends
at the incision of heaven and earth.
Who am I? Who am I?
Only silence meets my cry.

打着哈息的暮色

傍晚
暮色正向东走去
落日
留下的
是一抹弯弯的金弧
金灿灿的
一片凉意
在牧羊人的心里
打着哈息
傍晚
暮色正向东走去
伴着懒散的双腿
打着哈息
向东走去

Yawning Twilight

At nightfall
twilight shifts to the east.
The falling sun
leaves behind
a touch of sinuous gold.
Shiny gold,
the hint of a chill
in the shepherd's heart
is yawning.
At dusk,
twilight moves eastbound
on two sluggish legs
yawning
eastward, crawling.

我走进夜里

我走进夜里
去柴堆旁在零点里看天
村子里好亮
晚会的吹呼
村子的上空正在喧响
不远的邻村远远的好亮
天空里的星系低低的倾斜下来
无声的喧响　好亮
我真想　就是站在除夕的门口
看村子
今夜好亮
心里静静的喧响
直到夜的冰凉
这才跑进户内炉火正旺

I Entered the Midnight

I entered the midnight
to watch the sky by a haystack.
The village was alight
with loud revelers
filling the sky with their loud voices.
A neighboring village was also aglow
The glitter of stars low on a tilting sky
silent screams, piercing light.
I wished I were standing by the year-end gate
to observe the village in celebration.
How bright is tonight.
In my quiet heart beats a silent drum roll.
I know the night will be deep and cold.
I hasten inside where the stove glows brightly.

在这静静的小村旁

在这静静的小村旁
一个少女的脸在坐着沉思
默默地思索生活的路长
在这样的油画里
路人几回首
从不远处的庄稼地里
走来一个青年
正斜挎着袋子里的草
直直的走进村里
只是远远看了一眼村边的恋人
儿童和羊羔
那副快要掉的近视镜上
沾满了风尘　一个小村旁
一上午的时光

By the Quiet Little Village

By the quiet little village
a young woman sat deep in thought
quietly pondering the long road of life.
In this oil painting
passersby kept looking back.
From a nearby field
came a young man
with a hay sack across his shoulders
heading straight into the village.
Stealing a look only from afar at his desire:
kids and lambs.
That pair of dangling spectacles
was covered with dust. By a small village
this consumed the entire morning.

我睡不着了

我睡不着了
让灯就那么亮着
想到傍晚时
门前滚过一个大大的影子
我追了过去
好大一株棉蓬
像一艘飞船
搁浅在猪圈的坑旁
落日还留着一丝黄黄的发梢
我确没有瞭望到你的归来[13]
归来
暮色伴着我回到户内
伴着我孤独起伏的炉火
在永恒的冬日

---

[13] 这里的"你的"指的是作者的母亲。

Insomnia

My insomnia
keeps my night oil burning
when reaching the thought of twilight
I spot a shadow rolling by the gate.
I run after it
to face a big ball of cotton sheet
like a sail
stranded at the pigsty.
The setting sun is still wearing a bit of yellow hair
yet I failed to notice your homecoming[13]
return.
Twilight follows me into my hut
accompanying the lonely flickering flame
in an everlasting wintry day.

[13] Here "your" is used to address the poet's mother. See also p. 21.

天开了

可是我说了
门口有天开了
开在傍晚里
那日小儿说门口有天不开
我真担心天真的有一天
永远不开的时候
我真的不知如何面对
我们总要聆听来自天籁之音
我们总要聆听来自地籁之响
我们总要在西墙根里照一照橙色的光
我想没有哪一个人
不想知道天里的感觉
看门口天开了
无尽的彩霞

Opening Sky

But I said
by the gate the sky had opened up
in the twilight.
That day the little one said the sky by the gate didn't open up
I was worried that his naiveté would truly one day
stop the sky from opening.
I had no idea how to face it.
We always need to listen to the music of heaven
we always need to hear the din of hell
we always need to catch the orange light by the western wall.
I doubt anyone wouldn't
want to know how it feels in heaven
watching the sky open up by the gate
endless colorful clouds.

锁在抽屉里珍藏

农夫喜欢走在淡的静的静光里
步着诗的长度
和赶着羊儿的情愫
走过亮亮的场
走过亮亮的房舍
走过亮亮的电线外的
夕阳静圆的影子
眸子里眯缝着笑意
等到归来时
院中盆儿已被黄狗儿添光
听着进栏的羊儿
正撞着暖暖厚实的土墙　嗵嗵响
农夫走进户内把一串长长的诗行
微缩成一根亮亮的发丝锁在抽屉里珍藏

Treasure Locked in a Drawer

The farmer likes to walk in the faint, quiet, quiet light
gauging poetic meters with his steps
measuring his feelings about sheep herding.
Passing by the bright square
leaving behind well-lit homes
rounding the corners of lamp posts
beyond, the shadows of the setting sun
he squints to contain his pleasure.
Upon returning home
watching his dog empty its feeding bowl
listening to his sheep
bumping into their pen walls, clunk, clunk
entering his home, he shrinks a string of long poetic lines
into a shiny strand of hair securely locked inside a drawer.

在通往村子里的土路上走进黄昏

傍晚风尘中的一轮皎洁的

宛若月亮的落日呈着白色

在我的村西的小山头上等待着黄昏

风尘中的羊群簇拥着

在我的村旁的绿草地上等待着黄昏

傍晚风尘中的牧羊人

正眯缝着徘徊的眸子

在我的村旁的小山坡上等待着黄昏

风尘中的暮色宛如阴云蹒跚着

在我的村子的上空等待着黄昏

风尘中的村子被电线网着

无声地等待着黄昏

风尘中的几个农人走出麦田来扛着锄

在通往村子的土路上走进黄昏依此走进黄昏

Entering Sunset on a Country Road

A sickle of moon in the dusty twilight
as if the setting sun, veiled in white,
waited at the top of a western hill.
My sheep form a circle in the breeze
anticipating the setting sun on the village green.
The shepherd in the sun-lit motes
blinks clean his shifting eyeballs
waiting for day's end over the village hill.
Today's twilight dances like clouds lifted by the sand-strewn
    wind
waiting for the sunset in silence.
The village is shrouded in dust and electric wires
silently waiting for the sunset.
Out of the dust came a few peasants shouldering their tools
One by one entering the sunset on the country road to the
    village.

无声里各自静对着呼吸

我在夜的七点
站在毡门帘下
看两小儿在院角小解
看黑黢黢院的空间廓落
网着一个蓝青青的天幕
最亮的一颗星在厨房顶上
院面的晒绳上凉着衣物
一个个硬硬薄薄的表情
残雪在葵杆旁依着夜也依着
收缩着天际里橙黄色的天幕
猪儿还在暗处
食着夜的衣没完
好一个腊的暗淡的夜
无声里各自静对着呼吸

In Silence They Breathe

At seven in the evening
I stand under the felt door curtain
watching two little ones taking a leak
regarding the dark, empty spatial outline
that has enveloped the grey curtain of the sky.
The brightest star is over the kitchen roof
and a few clothes are drying on a string
each stiff and thin.
The remains of yesterday's snow huddle by the sunflower stalks
sucking in the sky's reddish yellow.
Pigs are hiding in the dark
endlessly squealing while feeding;
what an end-of-year twilight
in silent stares, each exhaling its silent breath.

划起那厚厚的草屑

划起那厚厚的草屑
我追寻在庄稼地边
寻找雨水
走过的足迹
我在走
我在寻走走在村外
划起那厚厚的草屑
拾起遗落的足迹
踩着雨水的影子
走过草地
我在寻走
我在走
遭到无常的追逐
划起那厚厚的草屑

Stirring up the Grass Clippings

Stirring up the grass clippings
I chase after the field
looking for rainwater.
Over yesteryear's footprints
I search
reaching the edge of the village
stirring up grass clippings
scooping up lost footsteps
stepping over the rain's shadow
over the grassland.
I search
searching
being chased after at times
stirring up the heavy grass clippings.

依恋成伤

我独自静立
至之暮色暗淡成青灰色
我知道户内
已拉亮了灯光
我却在无奈
像那院角的几棵树
枯着心景无色里
诗呵 我的诗
在这个季节里
你是否已离我而去
我却在无奈
独自暗淡回首
告别夜
依恋成伤

Crestfallen

I stand in silence, alone
until dusk loses its color to darkish grey.
I am aware that inside
lights are already turned on.
I feel helpless
like the tree in the yard corner
bare, colorless.
Poetry, my poetry!
In this season
is it that you've left me behind?
Abandoned
I turn to bid
farewell to night
crestfallen.

104

梦中屋顶上

梦中我在自家的屋顶上
这南面的高坡上
我独自站在高高的村上
鸟瞰整个村子
看呀整个村子的屋顶在地平线上
在这秋的晨日里所有的炊烟
像酒精灯一样的燃烧
看呀我站在高高的屋顶
我在大喊把胸腔内的激情
喊成喷泉般的泪水
燃烧我整个身躯
燃烧在这炊烟的早晨
醒来独自思索
原来只是一个梦中屋顶

Dreaming over the Roof

In my dream I was on top of my house roof
over on the southern hill.
I stood on top of the village, alone
overlooking the whole town.
Wow, the roof tops of the entire town are level with the horizon
and all the chimneys this autumn morning
are smoking like gas lamps.
Look, I am on top of the tall roof
shouting out all the passion locked inside my chest
shedding my tears like a fountain
on fire, my whole body
burning in this morning of chimneys.
When I woke up
I realized it was all just a dream.

人到院落旁

日落大
天地小
远山清云彩秀
人在天涯
小村外土窖旁
沿着白色路看坡下
绿草地里村间正喧哗
羊儿回来了
天清月正白风儿爽
那村间几株浓的桃树杏树枣树
沙枣花儿香一会儿工夫
暮色正寂静人在寂静旁思夏
昂首看星看月看村间
人到院落旁

By the Side of a Yard

Cosmical setting sun
pint-size planet
distant mountain in clear, colorful cloud
person over the edge of earth.
By a cellar outside the little village
along a whitish road down the hill
cacophony over the green pastured hamlet
sheep returning.
Clear sky, well-positioned moon, refreshing wind
a few lush peach, apricot, and date trees
giving out a passing fragrance.
Calm twilight, quiet person thinking in silence
looking up suddenly to find the stars, the moon, and the hamlet
person returning to the side of the courtyard.

几日里无电

几日里无电坐在傍晚的门槛上
等落日后的恬静清新凉爽
等一弯月牙在西天里生长
等晚饭后夏日的暮色充斥村庄
今晚月正南任两小儿嬉戏身旁
听女人在室内独叹
面对着温柔和夜的陪伴
一个小小院落的聊天
想着开了的窖后的疲乏
看月牙儿光金亮
看屋檐下的月光一片
憩息在长长的葵杆旁
看狗儿的黄色从院门口进来蜷缩无言
只听羊儿在房舍旁啃着暮色的声响

Power Out

Power is out now several days so I sit on the door sill
waiting for the cool air after sunset
a sickle of the rising moon in the western sky
and the summer twilight flooding the village.
Tonight's moon hangs directly over the southern sky,
    pampering kids' play.
I listen to wife's sighs inside
accompanied by the soft night
a small yard chit chat.
I think of my hard labor digging open the cellar
watching the golden moonlight
noticing a patch of white under the eave
licking the elongated sunflower stalk
observing the dog quietly rolling into the yard in a ball of yellow
and hearing the sheep chewing twilight under the eave.

彤彤落日

彤彤落日
彩霞飞翼
橙色里绯黄
变幻着又为绯红紫红血红
淡的绯墨
东天月儿淡
西天里
只剩红艳的一条彩裙
日落处
远山微微
隐显
绯兰的天空
村路正在暗淡里
隐显

Bright Sunset

Bright sunset
flying clouds
bright yellow inside orange
turning into blushing red, dark red, then blood red
darkened light black.
Slight trace of the moon over the eastern sky
the western sky
is left with only a colorful ribbon
where the sun sets.
A contour of a distant mountain
veiled
behind a reddish blue sky
the village descends into darkness
disappearing.

借书说

日落时从草场走回家园

女人去猪的圈里喂猪

叫我在灶旁喂火

米快烂了好撇起米汤

灶堂内闪着红色的火光映着室内暮色

我在灶旁喂火

蹲坐着等米烂了撇米

等疲倦慢慢褪脱出身躯

背后门口里走进女人我默默思索

回首原是黄生来借书一个村内后生[14]

说睡前有个习惯看上几页才睡得踏实

当我从高的书格内下来时

女人已拉亮了门的灯光

门灯下黄生已去才想起撇起米汤

---

[14] 此行引用清朝文学家袁枚创作的一篇散文《黄生借书说》中所述借书与读书的关系，着重强调认真读书的重要性。作者用自己亲身经历来阐述藏书人与借书人对读书的心里状态。有钱人拥有大量书籍，可是他们却不认真仔细去阅读它们；如果你无钱购买书籍，只好借书看，你则会很珍惜短暂拥有的机会，抓紧时间，认真阅读。张联在此始终以微妙的手法，描述出他个人从无到有的历程。就如袁枚一样，张联打开自家的书房大门，为他家乡贫穷的孩子们提供了一个精神避难所。

On Borrowing Books

Returning home from the threshing field at sunset,

I see my wife going to feed the pigs.

"Go feed the fireplace," she hollers.

"And the rice is about cooked."

The red flames in the fireplace are internecine with twilight.

I feed the fire

waiting for the rice to be fully cooked.

I slowly came out from my tired body

when I thought my wife came in from behind catching me
   dreaming.

Turned out it was a farmer's child who came to borrow a book[14]

telling me that bedtime reading makes him sleep better.

When I came down from my bookshelf ladder

My wife had already turned on the lamps.

Only then did I realize that I had left the rice cooker
   unattended.

---

[14] The line alludes to a Qing dynasty essay by Yuan Mei (袁枚) that recounts the story of a poor student who came to Master Yuan to borrow a book. Upon lending the volume, the master observes, "A book must be borrowed to be read thoroughly" (书非借不能读也). The essay subtly satirizes wealthy bibliophiles who might have large libraries of valuable books that he doubts they ever read closely or with passion. "When you borrow a book, you want to devour it. You will memorize everything you have read." This attests to Yuan's own experience of poverty (as well as to Zhang's), when a more prosperous neighbor was not generous enough to trust him with a book. Yuan would dream about borrowing them. Now that he has the means to collect books, he wants to make sure that his poor students can read any volume they want. Zhang Lian subtly invokes this scene to imply his own journey from a poor farmer who could not afford books or notepads to owning his current library, which, like that of Master Yuan, is a resource and refuge for rural children for whom the poet is an inspiring example.

陪猪儿进食

西天下青灰色的云霞里
正掩映着落日的一点红意
我走在村落间
只见几个闲人在一户院门口谈着宁静
在柔和的光里依着平静的房舍
谈笑丝丝凉爽的南风
圈旁堆积着新鲜的湿土粪
我寻觅东西不见骡儿归来
却在宁静里只见傍晚中　阔步思绪
须臾间回首只见傍晚里那村西口
一枚硕大的红色古币　正诠释
只是在透红透红里
走回时女人正静静在院落里
陪猪儿进食

Tending the Pigs at Mealtime

Into the ashen grey cloud lowering over the western sky
seeps a touch of red.
Walking through the village
by a courtyard gate I eavesdrop on idle chat.
In the dim light, by a peaceful home
their goodhearted laughter rides out to me like a cool breeze.
Fresh manure piles up by the donkey's barn
I fail to trace their return.
My thoughts pick up the pace in the quietude of twilight,
when I suddenly turn to spot by the village gate
a gigantic red coin, bathing the past
in its deep rosy glow.
Upon my return, I see my wife quietly
tending our pigs at mealtime.

走在炊烟里

晨日里
霜正白
走在村间
追逐骡儿向村外
旭日村东里
踩着暖暖酥软的光儿
看
几个娃儿
上学去
看
一个等车人
在村口踩白
答一两句话
便走在炊烟里

Enveloped in Chimney Smoke

Early in the morning
frost was at its intense whiteness
through the village
I chased after my donkey to the outskirts of the village.
With the rising sun in the east
I stepped on the soft, crunchy light
to observe
a few kids
on their way to school
to take in the sight of
a person waiting for public transportation
stamping his feet in the snow at the edge of town.
Exchanging a few words
I went on my way into the chimney smoke.

四月的天空里

看吧 四月的天空里
我的绿色村间
一片片的绿色在渲染
看哪 一个个无声的绿色
桃儿 杏儿 枣儿
看哪 一个个走动的绿色
驼儿梨儿骡儿羊儿鸡儿
在这四月的天空里
看哪 一个个微笑的绿色
房儿墙儿场儿路儿空气儿
看哪 我们的绿色村间
虫儿鸟儿小草儿人儿
一个个静止的绿色
在四月的天空里

April Sky

Look, the April sky
my plush village
bundles of green spread to dye.
Look, each noiseless green
peaches, apricots, dates.
Look, each moving green
tractors, plows, donkeys, sheep, and chickens
in the April sky.
Look, each smiling green
houses, walls, squares, roads, and air.
Look, our green village
bugs, birds, grass, and persons
each stationary green
in the April sky.

沉思里活动

雨后阴阴的云层
湿的小村
闲人在自家园子里院子里
无声地活动 构筑家园里的声音
静寂的活动
园旁的绿草丛小羊在咩叫
只是在埋首里沉思地活动
平整新建房的屋基
施肥地膜里的玉米
阴阴地云层 湿湿的小村
嫩绿的草地静寂的声音
时空里无声的延续
只是在埋首里 埋首里静寂
沉思里活动

Stirring in Deep Thought

Low dark clouds after the rain
dampened the village.
An idler in the yard
silently fixing his house to create a sound-filled home.
Quiet movements
bleating lambs grazing on the green pasture
I buried my head in deep thoughts.
Leveling the foundation for a new house
spreading manure to fatten the corn harvest
low, dark clouds, moist village
silently the green pasture rustled.
Time moves forward, space expands
deeply buried in thoughts
agitating in meditation.

冬季里

冬季里
农人终于静下心来
独自守着小屋
围着炉火
烤着芋
和一张桌
静静的伴着
两小儿的嬉闹
和妻的沉默
在家的氛围里
慢慢展开自己的思绪
偶尔的走出小屋
踏着暖的阳静的院落
聆听院门外的夕阳

Winter

Wintertime
when the farmer is finally able to relax a little
sitting in the house alone
by the stove
roasting a yam.
A table
silently accompanies
two little kids, playing
while his wife makes no sound.
In the homey atmosphere
slowly the farmer expands his thoughts
every now and then he steps outside
in the warm sun, the quiet yard
listening to the twilight sun by the gate.

慢慢的走来

静的小村里偶尔有几声鞭炮响
这年的三十
淡淡的蓝的空间这个十五日
淡淡的夕阳光正悄悄走动
去寻索日子在温馨里
闲人正独自走在晚饭后
在院落间昂首
看春的天似院角的几株润湿的树冠
仰望着春的天温蓄着情愫
一点点的生长
只见那西北里的天门打开
一抹淡洁的云彩
在整个净空里独自幻化着
慢慢的走来

Slowly Approaching

Occasional firecrackers go off in the otherwise quiet village
this New Year's eve
on the fifteenth of the Gregorian month with light blue sky
with shushed movement of the faint setting sunlight.
In search of the warmth of the day
the idler is taking a solitary constitutional
facing up to the sky
observing a few crown blossoms of the courtyard trees
taking in the warm feelings of the spring
climbing slowly;
perceiving a wide-open gate to the northwest sky
a touch of tinted cloud
enchantingly alone in the clear space
slowly approaching.

泥巴漆刷了的双脚

我的喊声驱赶着牲口
驱赶着青色的雾噼噼啪啪的响
驱赶着沟叉内的寂静
铁的犁儿的喊声
驱赶着我
驱赶着一粒粒黄色的土粒
熟透在噼噼啪啪的声里
翻飞着又静止
秋雾在沟旁的电线下噼噼啪啪的响
头发里溢着潺湿的雾汗
像狗舌头一样
舔食着我冰凉的面颊
沉重的
是那被心爱的泥巴漆刷了的双脚

Mud-caked Feet

My loud holler goads the donkey forward
causing the heavy fog to scream
moving silence out of the ditches.
The iron plow's bellow
propels me
turning each grain of the yellow earth
into flying songs
dancing then settling.
Autumn fog cries over the ditchside power line
and my hair emits a musty smell
like a dog's tongue
licking my cool face.
Heavily weighty
is that pair of feet caked in the cherished mud.

太阳黄黄的落着

太阳黄黄的落着
我和女人两小儿和车
在葵地里拾掇葵杆
在这个十二月十八日的傍晚
暖暖的冬日里赶着拉葵 葵的杆
一个男人和一个女人正忙着
可两小儿伏着地面
太阳黄黄的落着
暮色在淡淡的黄光里加深
南天里有几缕绯红的云彩
无声的嬉笑里
暮色在宁静着
两小儿制造着兔穴 兔穴里
太阳黄黄的落着

The Golden Sun Is Setting

The golden sun sets spreading yellow—
I, wife, and two children
together collect sunflower stalks.
On this evening of December eighteenth
a warm winter day we cart home the stalks.
One man, one woman, they busy themselves
with two kids rolling in the field
and the golden setting sun.
Twilight darkens in the yellow glow
against a few red clouds in the southern sky.
Amidst quiet laughter
twilight settles in peace
the kids dug rabbit holes,
in which the sun sets a spread of yellow.

十一月十五的初夜里

这个冬的农历十一月十五日的初夜里

我和两个小儿从老屋里出来

走过白色的场

东天里一轮橙色的圆月正爬上墙头

清淡淡的依着村旁

宁静里

村落间已无人走动

两小儿询问着玄机[15]

而西天里正萎缩着橙色天际里

映衬着青蓝蓝的天色

在干的空里沉默着

院门口的葵垛里正传出夜的呼吸

我和两小儿拾着鞋声

在院落里看初夜里的宁静

---

[15] 这首诗的意境是根据十五夜月正圆时的气场和天光的来临，进行画面推进的。"村落间已无人走动"强调村子的宁静和神秘来临之际，也可以说也正是神的出现，天象的吉祥呈现瑞光色彩和幻象的同时，此刻，诗人和小儿的出现走在神性的气场里。张联解释道："我自然知道这样的天机而不说，借用小儿之口的询问来明示玄机已出现。"

November Fifteenth Early Evening

This winter's November fifteenth early evening
I exit our old house with my two little ones
through a white square
while a wintry orangey moon is climbing over the wall
quietly clinging to the village.
In this peaceful space
there is no disturbance in the village
only the kids' questions about the mysterious state of being.[15]
Yet the western sky dissolves into the golden horizon
against the dark blue sky
silence in the dry atmosphere.
The sunflower stack emits night breaths by the courtyard gate
and me with the two little ones picking up our footstep noises.
In the yard we watch the silent night.

[15] Explaining the "mysterious state of being," Zhang Lian described his belief in a pure, higher power that comes to his aid when he is searching for words to express his often transient thoughts about the broader scheme of things, regardless of local or temporal conditions, rather from an eternal perspective. "This poem has two angles: the close-up shots of our physical surroundings such as my yard, the sunflower stalks, weather impact on crops, etc.; then the camera pans out to reveal the ever-so-powerful spiritual space where poetry takes place. The moon is married with that space to provide a tranquil moment for my thoughts to be captured in words that unite our daily physical life with the spiritual, thus making this fleeting moment eternal in words. I feel that divine moment, but I want it to be uttered through the mouths of innocents."

剪葵头

那日秋夜里
我在院子里剪下葵杆上的葵头
夜莺在半个音节里
从屋顶飞过
女人在户内敲葵
只是一种嘭嘭的声响
一个个萎缩着黝黑的葵头
正在一个过程中
嘎巴嘎巴里独自跌落
这样的秋夜里
小村独明
房在醒着
我剪下葵头送进户内给女人
单调里夜在宁静

Sunflower Harvest

That autumn night
I was shearing the sunflower heads in the yard
when a nightingale flew over the roof
in mid-syllable.
Woman was beating the sunflower heads inside
making *pong pong* sounds.
Each dry shiny black head
in the process
was noisily falling, individually.
This autumn night
my village is lit, alone
my house is awake.
I cut off the sunflower heads to pass to my woman inside.
Night is silent in this monotony.

落日终隐去

那日傍晚
淡淡的一轮橙色的落日
在天边的入口处　逗留
在这几日里的阴雨后
青紫紫的云系天空下
我和父亲看着落日的橙色
在村旁草地拉骡儿回去
感叹落日偏南半里
感叹秋草枯短
感叹阴云东北退去
感叹湿湿的村子在坡下沉寂
感叹日月如梭时光流短
青紫紫的天空下
落日终隐去

The Setting Sun Disappears

That twilight
a faint ball of golden setting sun
lingers at the entrance of the sky.
After a few cloudy and rainy days
bluish violet clouds form a band in the sky.
Father and I stare at the orange setting sun
while dragging our donkeys home.
We sigh about the skewed southern position of the setting sun,
lamenting the autumn grass shriveling short
bemoaning the dark clouds retreating to the northeast
mourning the quiet disappearance of the sodden village
grieving the ephemeral months and the fleeting time.
Under the blueish purple sky
the setting sun finally disappears.

这移动着的紫黄色 [16]

只见这移动着的紫黄色

上了小车

上了这木质的小车

然后淹晒在院门口的阳光里

让风儿去舔食

那秋日里的伤口

让伤口慢慢的干硬收缩

我移动着紫黄在院落里

有换苹果车驰过

女儿在哭泣

葵在院子里堆积

这个秋的傍晚里

我正在忙碌紫黄

装载潮湿压抑的暮色

---

[16] "紫黄色"指葵花籽脱掉后的葵头，这样一个壳的死亡，和生命诞生的分离的两个过程。在秋阳光下不断干瘪时的颜色是指生命失去时的过程中，那种物的颜色变幻痛苦和压抑的过程！另一边葵花籽新生命如婴儿般躺在打谷场上鲜亮地晾晒着。这样从物到人去思考死亡这样一个主题的探索和亲眼感受体验的时光。

This Mobile Purple Yellow[16]

Spotting the mobile purple yellow
climbing onto a cart
onto this wooden cart
then drowning in the yard gate sun
letting the breeze lick
that autumn wound
allowing the wound to slowly dry and shrink
I move the purple yellow in the yard.
An apple truck passes by
my daughter is crying
sunflowers pile up in the yard.
This autumn evening
I busily move the purple yellow
loading the damp, gloomy nightfall.

[16] "Purple yellow" describes the colors of the sunflower's head after most of the petals and seeds drop. The natural metaphor alludes to the intertwined human life cycles of death and birth, decay, and germination. The bloom fades and dries up in the sun, an emblem of the inevitable decline of the human body. As with the paintings of sunflowers by Vincent Van Gogh, the image reminds us of the suffering that follows beauty and offers a vehicle for mourning a loved one's death. At the same time, it promises regeneration, a new life is born as the seeds sprout and take root. The new crop once again rises from the soil to bask in the sun like the babies resting alongside their families bringing in the harvest.

落日

落日

在黄的浑圆里

沉默在青紫的光里

我正驱车向东而去

归来

你也在归来

在青紫的暮光里

闪烁最平静的面颊

我在回首里

保持最平静的沉默

在沉思里

让时间在最平静的暗光里度过

落日在黄的浑圆里闪烁

在青紫紫的暮光里

The Setting Sun

The setting sun
inside a dimly rounded yellow ball
quietly floating in the black-purplish light.
I was driving my cart east
returning,
so are you,
in the deep purplish twilight
a flicker in that calm face.
I turn my head
trying to keep my composure
deep in thought.
Time passes by in the most serene dim light
the setting sun shines through the yellow ball
through the purplish twilight.

看着栏内暮色隐藏

这个日子里
母亲给了我一株树
我种在院落旁
那是一株苹果树的幼苗
我试肥浇水后
便在春日的困意里
小睡
妻却缠扰着睡意
要去为幼苗栽葵杆
在半个院落的暮光里
围起了葵栏
在几行葱绿旁
我和女人
看着栏内暮色隐藏

Watching the Hiding Twilight

On this day
Mom gave me a tree
which I planted in the yard.
That was a young apple sapling
which I watered and fertilized.
In a sleep-inducing spring
a little nap.
Wife was nagging me
to plant sunflowers
in the half yard twilight.
Sunflower stalks as fences
by a few rows of green,
I and wife
watch the twilight hide in the fences.

闲人在院中独愣

我和小儿在院中嬉戏
不觉抬首
平视西天口
只见溅起几朵淡青青的云彩
这些陪衬的云朵呵
怎知日落后
却开放着蒲公英的花朵
在这夜的首里
静的淡的青的灰的花
在西天口
在小村旁
抒写一个白日后的暮色苍茫
在静的夜首里
闲人在院中独愣

The Lonely Distracted Idler

My child and I were playing in the yard
when I lifted my head by chance.
Leveling my stare over the western horizon
I spotted a few scattered light clouds.
These backstage clouds
how they, after the sunset,
like dandelions, gathered in a patch of blossoms!
At the beginning of such a night
quiet, light, grey cloud flowers
over the western sky
by the little village
present a vast twilight after a bright day.
At the start of a silent night
the distracted idler stood, alone.

冬日里

冬日里

窗外下着小雪在暮色里

户内我围着炉火烤芋

和家人一起

电视里

正演着《费家有女》[17]

偶尔出去小解

看着满院的雪

想着静静独居

羊儿要填草

不觉已在冬日里

围着炉火烤芋

就上几口闲情异趣

静静独居

---

[17] 《费家有女》是一部电视剧，是一部很温馨的剧本。费家有个好女儿，非常孝敬老人。这部电视剧也是针对现今中国年轻一代人的教育宣传片。中国政府根据近来国家出现的不孝子女问题设立了新法规，对虐待老人的子女大力惩罚，除了金钱赔偿外，不孝子孙还要服刑。

Winter

This winter evening
through the window I watch the light snow falling
while huddled by the stove we roast yams.
Together we watch
a television show,
"The Fei Family's Daughter." [17]
Every now and then, I go out to relieve myself
and become immersed in the snow.
I reflect on our isolated lives:
sheep at their feed
winter's imperceptible arrival
yams softening over the heat.
We gather in a feeling of relaxation
a contented, self-contained way of life.

[17] A popular TV series featuring a farm family whose daughter is dutiful to a fault. In today's China, where the traditional social norm of filial piety is fast disappearing, the government instituted a law that punishes children who fail to take care of their elders. This TV series was part of a propaganda campaign aimed at convincing the young to take more seriously their duties to their parents, community, and country. Any selfishness for personal comfort is discouraged as a break from the accepted moral code.

挑穿着暮色

那日里
暮色暗淡
我在院子里挑葵
把葵头挑上车去
这些脱去了葵的外壳
在这阴沉潮湿的傍晚里
让暮色浸透外壳
变得紫黄紫黄
胡乱地堆积在院落里
院落的每一个地方
闲人
在潮湿的压抑里
挑穿着暮色
挑出诗意

Teasing Open Twilight

That day
the dusk was dim.
I was picking sunflower seeds in the yard
then loading the stalks on a cart.
The pitted sunflower heads
on this dank, damp evening
absorb the twilight
turned into purplish yellow
haphazardly spread
all over the yard.
The idler
in the oppressive dampness
poking at the twilight
picking out the sense in gathering poetry.

148

走动成夜色浓发

我在门前的窖上吊水
去浇灌家园 这是村的运动
在自家园里低首时看那西天
此时地为上天为下
看那落日浑圆在彤彤红意里
爬上岸边
那蓝色的湖里
一片绛紫绛黄
让那淡淡红色弥满整个家园
东天里有大鹏展翅
这青色的云霞在淡默里沉寂
中天下的小村渐渐沉寂
闲人走动 走动成暮色苍茫
走动成夜色浓发

Turning into a Head of Thick Hair

I was bending over my family well to crank up buckets of
    water
for the irrigation of the crops, a routine village activity.
When I twisted my head, I saw the western sky
but the field was up and the sky down.
The ball of the setting sun blushed bright red
as it climbed over the bank
dying the blue water
a purplish yellow
spilling its redness all over the village.
Rooks spread their wings in the winter sky
black clouds settled in serenity,
the little village floated silently mid-sky,
the idler waddled toward the vast twilight
into the thick mane of the night.

瓜地

陌生的村旁有瓜地
地里有闲人各自半掩着面
让暮色在瓜地里乘凉
在明明暗暗里静寂着
我驱向东天
穿越暮色穿越乡间穿越大片的田野
这就是家园
多么清闲适宜地就着暮色
咬上一口西瓜 万籁俱寂
在这大自然的沐浴里
月儿在东天里爬上了岸
在暗红里羞涩一张硕大的脸
几声蛐蛐声来吹响了夏夜的幽曲
在这短笛声里度过这六月十六夜

A Melon Field

There was a melon patch by the unfamiliar village
and some idlers in the field veiled half their faces
shading against the twilight on the vines
playing hide and seek quietly.
I drive to the east
through twilight, through the village and across broad tracts
    of farmland.
This is my homeland!
What an apt leisurely moment at twilight
along with a slice of watermelon in the ubiquitous silence
bathing in nature.
The moon climbed over the horizon
dark red she showed a huge blushing face,
crickets sing to open the serenade.
In the nocturne of enchanting flute music, I spend the
    sixteenth of the sixth month.

无语里让那叶儿响

无语里让那叶儿响
似雨的声确又无雨
昨日傍晚里天穹飘动着云
在青黯色里
我在闷热里走出户外
光着膀子在葵里走动
爱抚着葵 想着雨
看那落日在橙色里闪烁
浑圆中浸在青云里
好似火 怎知夜色来临时
院面里溅着雨星
夜梦里听雨声响
很欣慰地翻身
很酣甜地熟睡

Leave Leafy Noise Alone

Let the leaves make their noise in silence
like the sound of rain when there is no rain.
Last night's moving clouds
drifted in darkness.
I stepped outside, leaving the stifling heat inside the house
pacing back and forth, bare-chested
thinking of the rain lovingly
watching the setting sun through the orange yellow
a floating, radiant sphere in the blue-green clouds
like a ball of fire foretelling the fall of night
a few glints of rain droplets in the yard
lulling me into a sound sleep
turning contentedly
sleeping tightly.

来振撼我的诗心

你看这千丝万缕　万缕千丝

这万束的青丝

这万束的纯洁和贞爱

在这一刻聚集汇合在一起

这是谁

这是谁

何以剪下了万束少女的青丝柔发

在这里飘逸

还是隐匿

这隐匿了的天真和纯洁

闪烁着万束的霞迹

我触摸这千丝万缕　万缕千丝

谁让这无数的贞爱

来振撼我的诗心

Let It Shake My Poetic Heart

Look at the thousands of threads and threads of thousands
the thousands of dark threads
the tens of thousands of trace elements of purity and love
at this moment they gather together.
Who is this?
Who is it?
Why does he cut off tens of thousands of the girl's black hairs
and let them float
or hide
this hidden naiveté and purity
as shiny as thousands of cloud shreds?
I ran my hands along the tens of thousands of threads.
Who allowed the infinite pure love
to shake my poetic heart?

走动着走向静的房

这样一幅的画在暮色里
婆婆和有身孕的媳妇
沿着村外路
在这初秋里
落日艳红着溅落村旁
溅起霞光万道
辉映着硕大的空间
让村落宁静着葵样的金黄
只见那新媳妇掂着肚子
拉着骡儿在暮色苍茫里
似剪影般默默移动着
婆婆在身后的一段距离里
让生活在时空的规律里走动着
走动着走向静的房

Approaching a Quiet Room

A family vignette framed in twilight:
mother-in-law and pregnant wife
along a road on the outskirts
in early autumn.
The setting sun casts red shadows by the village
scattering the colorful shards of light by the tens of thousands
reflected in the huge sky
silencing the region into a sunflower yellow.
I see my wife holding her belly
tugging at the donkey's reins in the expanse of dusk
like a shadow play moving silently
my mother-in-law a few steps behind
allowing a space where life moves according to its natural
    rhythm
edging toward a quiet room.

伴着暮色进入户内

伴着暮色进入户内
在这初秋的月夜里
静寂着
我透过窗玻璃
去窥视天体
在皎洁的月华里[18]
一枝葵的花朵飞行着而来
尾随着
一轮葵样的光彩的太阳
在静淡的红色里
沿着低空里飞行
谁的神来之笔才能临摹这幅
油彩画 我看这寂静的天体
在这梦的初秋的月夜里 静寂着

---

[18] 张联解释说："月华"指月光从天空上照下来的光彩。后面一句"我看这寂静的天体"是这首诗意境的故事和奇景，发生就是来自天体，或者说是来自神的启示，让诗人在沉默中思考和预示什么秘密的来临。

Entering the House in Twilight

Entering the house
in this early autumn twilight
silence.
I look through the glass window
to sneak a peek at the galaxy
in the bright moon magnificence.[18]
A sunflower petal floating by
following
a sunflower-like colorful sunset
in the quiet redness
flying low along the sky.
Whose magic brush can paint in oil
such a landscape? I observe this quiet celestial body
in its dreamlike early autumn moonlight, quietly existing.

[18] Queried about the apparent neologism "moon magnificence" (月华) in line six, Zhang Lian proudly replied that as a modern poet, he made up expressions and charted new territory in poetic diction. To reflect his originality, I have translated the expression using the original meaning of each word.

说这正是流光的时辰[19]

我在暗淡的暮光里
向东走去
迎面走来宽面宽眉的老者
叫我而去
说这正是流光的时辰
我回首 只见西天里的霞光流动
灰色的云彩
夕阳在淡白里渐渐沉寂
我和老者执拗在这落日的霞谷
老者挥袖长去
并让我把霞坡上的爬行物挥去
那些蜥蝎蟾蛉蜘蛛们
我让自语驱赶着土色的尤物
只是瞬息已向谷底隐去

The Moment of Moving Light[19]

In the dim twilight I
move eastward.
A square-jawed, bushy-eyebrowed elderly man approaches,
hollering at me to get over
saying now is the exact moment of the moving light.
Turning my head, I see colorful changes in the western sky:
Greyish clouds,
the setting sun drifts silently in the pale aether.
The old man and I attempt to contain the sunlight in the valley
when he, flinging his sleeve, leaves me
to shoo away all the bugs from the sun-lit slope
those crickets, beetles, ants and spiders.
I let nature do its own trick
and in no time they are on the valley floor.

19 根据诗人张联提供的资料，此诗创作时间是2000年左右。张联说这"也是我在小阳沟时期二十年，完成傍晚风格的白玉之塔和使命的一个最后逗留人间的徘徊时间！是特别受欧美文学思潮，对纯文学理念的观念的神圣的维护和尊严纯洁的保持。就是如斯蒂芬*茨威格著的《与魔鬼作斗争》一书对大诗人要求的理念，神性意义完成使命的纯洁离世，而不是小丑似的活在人间。而在这样的意义上，我与魔鬼作斗争的力，我与天意难违的力而抗争，对神性意义里天机的再次泄露！同时，提前预示我有能力驱赶那些蜥蜴蝎子蟾蜍蜘蛛们所象征的离开和消失！成为继续维护诗歌纯洁纯粹的大使而留世更久的伟大意义。"

19 A voracious reader, Zhang Lian draws inspiration from both classic Chinese literature and Western philosophy and literature. The year 2000 marked an important juncture in his writing career. After spending almost twenty years in Little Sunny Ditch composing the *Twilight* poems, Zhang Lian chanced upon a translation of the second volume of Stefan Zweig's *Master Builders* trilogy, an epochal work in which Zweig sketches a composite of the European mind through intellectual portraits of highly influential figures, including Hölderlin, Kleist, and Nietzsche. As Zweig ruminates on the mission of the poet, the sense of a vocation especially resonated with Zhang Lian, who deeply believes in the sanctity of ideas as expressed through poetic means. In this poem, the old man signifies a sacred soul that guides the poet's journey. The crickets, beetles, ants, and spiders are metaphors for the detritus of human waste as our appetite for material satisfaction consumes us. Zhang Lian subtly challenges the materialist society that has captured China's new generation while masking his own beliefs in this dream-like, surrealist fantasy of the old man's supernatural powers, ironically credible because it is so relevant to contemporary Chinese thought and society.

生命又在开始

想想不觉寒气已来
雪儿进入冬季
想那桔黄色的杏叶儿
在秋末里独自开放
村间真的只有杏的美
不管在村里还是村外
总有那样一两株两三株
独自儿辉煌 祥云般儿飘浮
偶尔的让秋风摘走了几片
凋零了几片 花瓣似的
在桔黄色里寂寂默默
留恋着秋色
在桔黄色的暗哑里
生命又在开始

A New Life Begins

Before you know it cold air has arrived
snow has ushered in winter.
The yellow apricot leaves
are in solitary bloom in the waning days of autumn—
there is really only the apricot beauty in the village.
No matter outside or inside the village
there are always a couple or a few blossoms
floating alone like magnificent clouds
every now and then allowing autumn to pick away a few petals
to wither the last remaining leaves.
In silence the orange yellow
reluctant to let autumn go
amid her rasping voice
vitality starts a new cycle.

滚动已很久远

你伴着暮色的身影
为何不隐去
确让那洁白和纯真
在单纯的颈项里
袒露
你看着什么呢
怎能让你的光芒
敛息在低首里
我的灵性的诗哟
在这傍晚的日子里
不期而遇
却又无期而失
你看那西南半里路呀[20]
滚动已很久远

---

[20] 中国的一里是一英里的三分之一

Been a Long Way Away

Accompanying the moon shadow, why
don't you disappear?
Instead you allow that pure white innocence
to rest on that chaste neck of yours
laid bare.
What are you looking at?
How can you allow your radiance
to muse in lowered shyness?
My magic poems
on this dusk-covered day
chance to meet you
then unexpectedly lose you!
Look, that southwestern half-li road[20]
has rolled already a long way away.

[20] One Chinese *li* is one-third of a mile.

傍晚的日子

傍晚的日子里
乘车而归
送走了那白蒺藜的梦
在思维里萦绕
你看这芸芸众生
框在一个时间里行走
我的迟钝的眸光里
触及诗的灵性
丽女
这样一个丽女
不管几千年降生一次
可是呵 你何以出现又降临
你难道不知在这混沌的时空里
如何适从

Days of Twilight

In the days of twilight
I return by public transportation
dispatching those phantoms of white herbs
lingering pensively.
Look at these people
walking, framed in that time zone.
In my dull gaze
I stumble on my poetic spirit.
Pretty woman
such a beauty
no matter in how many thousands of years she appears once.
But how can she appear and disappear?
Don't you know in this chaotic time and space
you need to adjust, pretty woman?

你去看吧

你去看吧
田野光秃秃
荒原一片枯萎
闲人走动
羊儿游来游去 麻雀儿喧哗着
村子一片宁静
桔黄色 桔黄色
我的思维儿寂长
等待着那雪花儿飘来
结伴儿
在午夜里飞舞
这是一场梦 一场桔黄色的梦
挥洒完时 我便悄悄儿裸露身心
献给了夜

Go Take a Look

Go take a look
at the fallow fields
an expanse of wilted wasteland
with an idler walking about
goats roaming and sparrows chirping
but the village in total quietude.
Yellowish yellow
my lonely thinking
waiting for snowflakes to come
coupling
floating in the middle of the night.
This is a dream, a yellow dream
thrown away. I expose my heart
to the night.

让谁暗淡成色

土的房和白色的场
静的声响
沉着　下沉着
深深的沉着
天色下沉
静静的响
我独自撑着天
看村间朦胧
我独自醒着
只是不见你的归来
我独自相思
天色下沉
静在响
让谁暗淡成色

Darkening into Color

Clay hut and white square
so quiet it sings.
Calmly descending
deeply serene
the sky is falling.
Quietly noisy
I alone hold up the sky
observing the village in haze.
I alone stay awake
without a trace of your return.
I alone am lovesick.
The sky is falling
so quietly that it sings
color into the darkness.

去追逐婧女的青睐

我走在纷乱和扰攘里
携带疾病
道士走来
让两位老者医治
用那似雷电的手指
先击穿我的大脑
然后捅击我的胸腔
击碎我的心　击碎我的肺
还有我的肝
让我在似痛非痛中
灼热
去趟过一条暮色的河　燃烧
我正在脱胎换骨　换骨脱胎
去追逐婧女的青睐

Chasing after Beauty

I pace in distraction and disturbance
carrying illness.
The Taoist priest comes over
asking the two doctors to diagnose
using those electrifying fingers
first poking through my brain
then pounding on my chest
probing my heart, piercing my lungs
plus my liver
leaving me in painless pain
calcinating
crossing a river at twilight, sweltering
reborn, I was
chasing after the favor of a girl.

日落后

当日落后
你在户内静坐
只是那么一刻钟里
你透过窗玻璃
看到南天里的飞彩
在绯黄里
你不觉惊异
走到户外
却是满天的飞彩
在绯黄里
而那西天里
却已绯红
在那绯红绯黄里
便是仙境

After Sunset

After sunset
you sit inside in silence.
Only at one moment
did you look out the window
and see the colorful clouds in the southern sky
shrouded in hazy yellow.
Surprised
you venture outside
to find the whole sky in color
hazy yellow all over.
Only in the western sky
the clouds already turned into bright red
and in that bright red
resides the wonderland.

升在北天上

而北天里衔接西天的
层层青云在浮起
而我这中天下的闲人
便就此坐了下来
守着院门口看天
看霞羽的变幻到飞失
那只是一些白色的飘羽
飞逸着
而半个月亮在银样地西飞
飘过银样的飞羽
看这村街上无数暮色声响
而那北天里的青灰色的云系
似扯幕般的升起
升在北天上

Up to the Northern Sky

And the northern sky connects with the western sky
where layers of clouds float
and me, the idler, in the middle sky
sitting
at the yard gate to observe
the clouds changing shape and disappearing
only a few white wings
floating, flying.
A half moon drifts to the west like a silver coin
floats over the coin-like clouds.
I take in the village's numerous muffled noises
and the northern sky's greyish clouds
rise up as if ripping open a stage curtain
to the northern sky.

须臾里

须臾里
一道无声的闪
我再看这雨的身躯
在一个小的天里
我只是惊异
而驾驭这雨的身躯的
青黑的幻形里
原是那千年的老龙[21]
弯曲着灰白的银须
昂着伟岸的龙冠
舞动着偌大的身躯
让那黑色的尾掩映着
暮色消沉在西天里
我看这老龙在行雨

---

[21] 在中国神话传说中，龙可以说是我们信仰中最为神圣的图腾了。自古至今，中华民族以龙的传人自称，早在《说文》就有龙的记载。龙是象征吉祥的动物。在神话作品中，有四海龙王的说法，每个方位的龙王与人世间的皇帝没有什么区别。龙有解人间干旱之苦的神力，在此诗中，张联引用《西游记》里的老龙行雨的传说，"一百零八点雨减数犯罪天条"来阐述这一刻小阳沟天空的雨意的神奇。

A Flashing Moment

In a blink
a flash of silent lightning
zips through the body of rain
and I, in the small universe where I reside,
open jawed, in awe
riding over the thicket of rain
make out a dark shadow
the thousand-year-old dragon[21]
twisting his whitish grey whisker
thrusting his crown
thrashing his gargantuan body
his epic tail whipping
the twilight mirrored in the western sky
I behold the ancient dragon calling down the rain.

---

[21] By far the most prominent of ancient totems in the Chinese mythic consciousness from its pre-historic origins, the dragon bears many meanings. Because it is claimed by emperors as the symbol of might and right, the Chinese proudly pronounce themselves its descendants. The dragon is described in *Shuo Wen* (说文), one of the earliest dictionaries of the Chinese language (c. 200 AD), as the benevolent creature who awakens nature's spring after hibernating in the deep sea, wielding his power to bring rain. Elaborating on classical Chinese literary tradition, Zhang Lian derives his allusion from the supernatural allegory of the *Journey to the West* (西遊記, Xī Yóu Jì) by Wu Cheng-en (吳承恩) published in 1590, in which the dragon is one of the main characters.

正敲响着冬的土地

当飞鸦和它的影子在沟畔上飞行时[22]
羊儿也就在不远处的
榆树林带间的茬地里温暖
黑色的背脊闪着墨绿色的阳光
静寂中听到的是寒风翻飞的声响
牧羊人在向阳的沟叉处
缩成一只白色的羊
聆听冬
在亮的残雪片上
湿润的自语
想像着黑色的美丽
和墨绿色的飞行
只见那点燃晚霞的喙
正敲响着冬的土地

Knocking Awake the Winter Land

The crows in flight cast shadows over the ditch,[22]
goats not far away
warm each other in the elm tree grove.
His darkened back turns the sunlight into dark green
a churning, chill wind breaks through silence
the goat herder at the sunny side of the ditch crossing
shrinks into a white sheep
listening to winter
over a remnant snowflake
talking to itself
dreaming of dark beauty
and the forest green flight
that sunset, glowing beak
is knocking awake the winter land.

²² 张联在他所有诗中所用的 "鸭儿," "飞鸭," 或者 "鸭子" 都指的是常规的乌鸦。诗人用 "鸭儿" 等词来代表乌鸦，意味着张联把自然界的野生动物描绘为驯服的家禽。由于长年累月的干旱，张联的家乡没有鸭子，诗中所用的鸭是诗人利用的一种亲昵法，也是他内心期望家乡能有荷塘溪水，鱼鸭戏水的景象。

²² Rather than "crows," Zhang Lian actually uses "duckling," "flying duck" or simply "ducks" in other Chinese versions of this poem. In the spirit of endearment even to the point of domestication, a wild crow is seen as tame as a duckling in a farmer's pond. The poet points out that due to year-round drought in his region, this linguistic manipulation is essentially wishful thinking, however tenuous a poetic justification of his belief. I used the word "crow" in translation to reflect the literal bird named in this text.

那天早晨

那天早晨
我收拾着芋窖
准备盛芋
在院子里的空间
听厨房里的女人
在叮当响
听孩子在闹
听鼓风机在吹着早晨
我心里便渗透着
对生活的热爱
不几天
芋又满窖
我好象就是芋
我在芋的窖内聆听

That Morning

That morning
I was cleaning up the cellar
to store harvested yams.
Across the space of the yard
I heard my wife in the kitchen
clattering pots and pans
along with kids' playing
and the bellows for the stove tooting a morning song.
My heart filled with
love for life.
In a few days
yams would fill the cellar
and I felt like the yams
at the bottom of the cellar, attentively listening.

准备归去

你知道了吧
我就是一个鸦儿
在暮色中独自拍着翅膀
才能美丽自己的身影
也许很丑在小村里有一个巢穴
独自珍爱着
让时光看得很平常
静静度过每一个很平常的日子
独自飞落静立
等待着　等待着
在院的墙头没有思想
只是一个影子
无声的伴着一片柔光静意
准备归去

Ready to Return

Do you already know
that I am a crow
flapping my shiny wings in twilight
to flaunt my beautiful shadow?
Or I am an ugly crow hiding inside the nest
cherishing myself
making the passing of time a routine
spending each day without much fuss?
Flying alone, landing solo
waiting, waiting
on top of the yard wall, dull
only a shadow
silently accompanying a patch of soft light
ready to return.

暮色已炸裂在卧雪的村庄

日落时南的天际里凉晒着紫色的网
这一刻我走动在冬的院落里
我知道神再一次向我示意
让那紫亮亮的一张硕大的网
在光速里穿越我沉默的眸光
或者说已明示了我多年的辛劳
已拥有一张织好了紫色的网
让他凉晒在冬日里的天体清寂中
沿着一层天的极蓝让时空曳着向东天里
滑行 在夜幕闭合时我已挥洒到天际
这一刻田野空旷我走动在冬天的院落里
只是在静的村落旁
暮色已炸裂在卧雪的村庄
我用整个胸襟感受着神的足迹

Explosion Over the Snow-Crouching Village

Purple netting dries in the cool air of the southern sky
while at this moment I am pacing in the wintry yard.
I see that heaven once again is showing me
how that purple-colored huge netting
at the speed of light penetrates the quiet morning
or expressing that years of my hard work
have woven a purple net
drying in the cool wintry celestial space
along an extreme blue sky, dragged east
gliding to the closing of night's curtain, to earth's end.
This moment witnesses a vast empty field, me pacing in the
    yard
so quiet by the village.
Twilight has exploded over the snow-crouching homes—
With my whole heart I take in God's heavenly trace.

一个个蠢动着的身影

农夫一个人踱着步
农夫走出来
一个人踱着步
向村间里走动
在青的淡泊宁静适宜中
村落里无人走动
农夫走在村街上
看看天
太阳和淡的云系
看看地
村落和几十棵榆树的哑然
只有几头春日里的童年小猪
蹭着墙根
一个个蠢动着的身影

Many a Scampering Shadow

The farmer counts his lonely steps—
Out he goes
one figure, pacing
toward the village.
In the dark yet clear and quiet air
no one moves about in the street.
The farmer on the main road
looks up at the sky
the sun and clouds
then down at the ground.
Silent village and trees
only a few spring piglets
rubbing against the wall—
a few scampering shadows.

你可否已在暗淡的声中归来

知道户内有炉火
思想你是否去了远方
那日里的班车上
你幻化成一个淑女静坐车上
独自闪烁着灵性
而我在痛苦里迟钝
不管哪一日里 我总要在户外张望
见西南天空里一片辉煌
一块硕大的黄色的云
独自站立着四射光芒
无数霞光流彩
和一片静的声响
暮色在村旁屏息
你可否已在暗淡的声中归来

Could You Have Returned from the Hushed Echo?

Knowing the stove is burning inside
I thought of your being far away.
That day on the shuttle bus
I imagined a young woman silently sitting
with her inner spiritual light
dwarfing me in my pain.
No matter which day I always look outside
to search for the southwestern sky's splendor:
a huge patch of yellow cloud
alone, upright, emitting light in all directions
numerous colorful clouds, moving
alongside an expanse of silent sound
dusk rests on the village edge.
Could you have returned from the hushed echo?

让思维啁啾在这白色的村间

户内两小儿吵闹

我寻觅静外

无奈走到户外

默读诗学

看西天里

纷披的青灰色的云系

像老屋里的

两株纷披着的树冠纷披着

有两三只麻雀飞来落在电线上

无意间啁啾几声

声下

是圈里羊儿的吃草声

谁似等待入巢迟迟

让思维啁啾在这白色的村间

Let Thoughts Sing in the Blanched Village

With two little ones fighting inside the house
reluctantly I venture outside
for peace
silently reading poetry while
watching the western sky and
a flock of floating, greyish clouds
like the old cottage
shrouded in the shadow of the treetops.
A couple of sparrows perched on the cable line
carelessly singing
under which
my goats bray in the yard
as if waiting to enter nests.
Let thoughts sing in the blanched village.

晨日里的小雪

晨日里的小雪
覆盖在旧雪上
旧雪里的村子
又在新雪上
寂上寂里的村子
在白的色里迷失
人从房子里出来的时候
一只鸦儿在村子里的
有雪的草垛上不语
这样的不语很好
因为它在我的院旁
静中静的两个影子
在这个世界里
无语真好

Snow in the Morning

The early morning snow
drifts over the old snow.
The village under the old snow
now is covered in a fresh layer.
The quiet village
is lost in the bright white color.
When a villager came out of the house
a crow is out there, too.
On top of a snow-covered haystack, no words
are so good when there is no word.
By my courtyard
two silent figures
in this world—
No word feels so right.

在一片白色里

在一片白色里
村人
在各扫着门前雪
静静的沙沙声
走到院落里
走在屋顶上
静静的
一片白色里的沙沙声
天空上的青韵里
透着淡淡的粉红色
裹着一个无色的晨阳
天地间好大好大的梦寐
村外走向青色韵致里的是几个童年
静静的静静的沙沙声沙沙声在响

In a Patch of Whiteness

In a patch of whiteness
villagers
each minding their own business
quietly rustle
out to the yard
up onto the roof
quietly
rustling in a patch of whiteness
while above the sky in its greenish rhythm
emerges the light dust of pink
wrapping around a pallid morning sun—
such a tremendous dream between heaven and earth.
Outside the village are a few youngsters walking into the
    green rhythm
silently rustling in a quiet susurrus.

在无风的静绿中

村旁的绿草地上
有几滩小羊啃着夏日里的小草
就着几个婆姨
就着绿色的闲聊
在无风的静绿中
这样的一个下午
看淡远的夏日在西天里
恬淡而飘逸
谈自家园中的瓜还是豆
谈新出闺的女儿的归来
就着这样的几个婆姨
就着这样的几滩小羊
就着这样的一个下午
在无风的静绿中

Amid a Windless Quiet Green

On the village green
a few sheep are safely grazing
while a few housewives
gossip in the shade
of a windless quiet green.
Such a summer afternoon
under the distant western summer sky—
a touch of ease, a hint of elegance.
What about my garden's melons or beans?
When is my married daughter returning home?
It is just so a few housewives
and a few sheep
on just such an afternoon
can take shelter in a windless quiet green . . .

黄色的豆角花

狗儿

卷着尾巴

太阳里

追逐

轻捷的风儿

鸡儿走动

鸽儿飞

玄鸟呢喃

在看见的

远远草色里

有暖暖的豆角花

我脚下的泥根里

不痴不痴

黄色的豆角花

Yellow Bean Blossoms

A dog
curled up his tail
in the sun.
Chasing
the light wind
birds jumping
doves flying
cooing.
What is seen
in the distant grass?
Warm beans flower
underfoot in the mud—
Not so wild
are yellow bean blossoms.

在冬的微雪羞光里

十点钟吧走出村口
我去牧场
在村外里踩着微雪 经过大片的
耕种地 温和的冬日上升着
在稀疏的村旁林边
一颗高大的榆叉上传来两对喜鹊儿的
叫声 这里是我的家园
羊儿在羊肠道里 急急地走动
或者是游动
把冬日拉得很短
去到井边从水槽里拾起淋漓的嘴唇
又踅转身 回到牧场里 在回头草里
捡拾昨天夜里沙鸡过夜的粪便
在冬的微雪羞光里

In the Coy Wintry Light

Out of the village at ten
on my way to the pasture
stomping over a large, bright snow-covered patch
in the pasture, earth's temperature rising
by the scattered grove.
Over a tall elm tree came the chirping of magpies
signaling the proximity of home.
Sheep moving quickly
or perhaps wriggling
stretching winter taut
over to the water trough to slurp a few mouths full
doubling back to the pasture
picking up last night's bird scat
in the coy wintry light.

微明的林间

冬日那天边退去的青雾
擎着白色的云层
你以银色装饰着
斑剥着的雪
你以银色装饰着
那幽暗的树冠
你以银色装饰着
那大片的荒原
你以银色装饰着
那一对嬉戏中鹊儿的颈
还有那雪地上的羊儿
正踩着斑剥着的雪
沐浴在冬日里的
微明的林间

Dim Forest

The retreating light fog at the edge of the winter sky
holding up white clouds
dressing up in silver
the mottled snow
as if adorned in silver
the dark treetops
as if plated in silver
large stretches of wasteland
as if clad in silver
neckties on the playful magpies
and the sheep over the snow-covered land
scampering over the mottled snow
bathing in the winter sun
dim forest.

夏日里

远处传来
一只乌鸦的
喘叫
像是在脑海的深处思考
看坡下
村子如卧
日班车正在经过
几簇幽暗的村冠下
那是茂盛的苗稼
有几多锄葵人的闲暇
淡淡云系
凉凉风
在这个清爽的
夏日里

Summertime

From far away
came the cry
of a crow.
As if thinking deeply
down the slope
the village seems crouched in anticipation
of the daily shuttle passing.
Beneath a few shadowy treetops
are bumper crops
and a few resting farmers
light clouds
cool breeze
on this temperate
summer day.

一首首没有展开的诗

我走进画室
一个不显眼的屋子
一个静静的画室
挂满一张张的画卷
风格各异
桌子 画具
一个俏瘦的身影
年轻的画师
在画卷上不停地
题着诗句
什么时候 我已走出画室
痴痴的手中
紧握一个长长的画卷
和一首首没有展开的诗

Each Unfinished Poem

I enter the nondescript studio
a plain and simple room
a quiet chamber
lined with paintings
in different styles
tools spread out on the table
a skinny shadow
the young painter
working nonstop, his brush oscillating
inscribing a colophon
unaware when I left the studio
in my hand
holding tight a long scroll
and each unfinished poem.

静默

淡淡的雪花儿飘着
纷纷扬扬
我在屋顶上
瞭落日
囚在乌云里
撒下一片红光
漫过所有的原野
和我炕的烟缕
我在屋顶上
瞭落日
和雪花儿的飘舞
囚在时空里
漫漫红光
静默

Quietude

Light snow floating
scattering
on top of the roof
I watch the setting sun
shrouded in dark clouds.
It spreads a patch of light
over the pasture
and illuminates my cellar's smoke.
Over the rooftop
I observe the setting sun
and the dancing snowflakes
imprisoned in time and space
patchy red
quietude.

我在黄昏的通道内停留[23]

我在黄昏的通道内停留

这里的街衢上

走动着纸的车辆

走动着无数的人群

杂乱 纷扰 无章

有陌生的和不陌生的

和我开着玩笑

或嬉或逗或戏或乐

正分吃节日的肉块

我默记街衢里的规矩

我沿着黄昏通道走出了街衢

牛头伴我步行到枯黄的草坪上

回首时 已化作一只白色的狗儿

微笑着离去

---

[23] 这首诗以魔幻超现实主义的手法来描述在梦境里天与地之间黄昏的那个切口，或者说是进入地狱的那个门口，那个通道。诗人引用但丁的《神曲》之意境，体现在不同的过程中经历有惊无险，而又被神力拯救！在每一层寻找自己！在现实生活的环境中，诗人张联目睹地域中被惩罚的所有罪恶，在写作过程张联在炼狱中寻找灵魂的洗礼和纯化，创作诗歌的同时，也是张联受到一次一次的洗礼过程，最后终于上升到天堂。

Hanging Around in a Tunnel[23]

At dusk I linger inside a tunnel.

On the roadway

are moving paper vehicles

roaming about are many people

chaotic, out of order

some familiar faces and some strangers

joking around

and pulling my leg

eating chunks of meat from festivities.

I remember road rules,

I walk out of the tunnel along the twilit sidewalk

a cow head accompanies me out to the withered grassland

turning my head, it has turned into a dog

sauntering away with a smile.

[23] This poem adopts a surrealistic approach to life's images even as it invokes Dante's *Divine Comedy* as a source of inspiration. Zhang Lian avers that life offers a glimpse of the sins that Dante catalogued in his "Inferno." He compares the writing stage of his life to the ascent along the mountain of Purgatory, poetically experiencing a path of purification. In the end, as with Dante, the poet rises to Heaven, partly due to the recognition of his poetry by readers and critics.

我的另一个魂魄²⁴

我的另一个魂魄
在黄昏通道
残叫 呻吟 跌落
我怜悯
我走了过去
翻过那座山
走进黄昏通道
牛头还是马面
正踩躏着我的另一魂魄
我恼恨 哀求冷冻
牛头说
需猫头鹰脑髓100克
香炉100盏白金纸100张
我的魂魄才不被惊扰

<hr/>

²⁴ 因为灵魂是由魂和魄组成，这里的魂魄是指另一个我的分身魄的游走，并在不断地去体验和感觉人间和地狱的秘密，如何从炼狱到地狱，在危险中自救或是来自神力的它救的故事，以及才能到达天堂的一个过程的思考和展现。

216

My Other Soul[24]

My other soul stays
in the tunnel at dusk
moaning, screaming, falling.
For mercy's sake
I go over
crossing the mountain
entering the twilit tunnel
cow head or horse face?
I ravage my doppelganger.
Annoyed, numbed, I make a plea
the cow head says,
"In need of 100 kilograms of an owl's brain membrane
100 incense burners and 100 sheets of white gold paper money
    to burn
to ensure the eternal sanctity of my soul."

[24] Like many Chinese, Zhang Lian believes there is an agonistic split between body and mind, a facet of the immensely important dichotomy of *yin* and *yang*. Our physical flesh and bones, or the yin, is considered the *po* (魄), whose existence relies on the *hun* (魂), the yang energy or spirit. In this poem, Zhang Lian describes how the physical body drifts away from the spirit to investigate the secrets of the living and the dead. It explores the journey to hell and purgatory, where it withstands the tests that Dante also relates in his epic *Divine Comedy*, which Zhang Lian read religiously. In this arduous journey, the soul is saved only by a supernatural power, reaching Heaven and, from this elevated perspective, gaining insight into the meaning of life.

询问谁那依此走过的

我走进寂静的通道[25]
神秘地躲藏在侧道内蜷缩
从通道的另一端传来
阴暗的气息神秘地走过
几只怪异的山羊
几只怪异的山狗
几头怪异的狼虫虎豹
我神秘地沿着侧道躲藏
开阔处
一座院落
一户人家
在寂静处喧哗
我静目在人家
询问谁那依此走过的

Who Once Walked this Path?

I enter the quiet tunnel[25]
stooping to hide in a side alcove.
From the other end of the tunnel
the dank air approaching
a few strange-looking goats
and bizarre wild dogs
more weird wolves, or tigers, or leopards.
I hide deep in the tunnel
in the opening
a courtyard
a family
making noise in a quiet place.
I stare at the family and wonder
who has passed along this road?

²⁵"通道" 指走向地狱里的路线，因身后另一端阳间的呼唤，又转身回来。"那依此走过的" 指那些象征着人间的走向地狱的一些不纯洁的灵魂。

²⁵ "Tunnel" refers to the path descending to hell or the *yin* side of existence. When the poet hears the call from the living, the *yang* of the dualistic concept so important to Chinese philosophy, he turns back, but not without contemplating the fate of those who have gone all the way to hell, whose souls have been burdened by impurity.

碰响着肩膀

冬日里的皮袄

大暖帽

一根棍子

走遍草场

在村外里

几个牧羊人

碰着肩膀

笑眯眯地

乜斜着对方

乜斜着天空

以及天空里的太阳

慢慢的向前缓缓地走动

在空旷里乜斜羊群

碰响着肩膀

Shoulder Bumping Noise

Winter coat
warm hat
a walking stick
pacing the square
outside the village
a few herders
rubbing shoulders
full of smiles
squinting at each other
peering at the sky
narrowing their eyes at the sun above
edging forward, slowly
looking for their sheep
noisily bumping shoulders.

我在那凝固着的湖边爬行

我在那凝固着的湖边爬行
穿梭在水草之间
远处有几条虎样的犬
它们能否和我一样
爬过湖面
又似
在高耸的山峰间走动
爬向另一侧峰巅
辉煌的是
绿色的峰巅正燃烧着
红色的火焰
照亮艰辛闪烁的云梯
在这很陡很陡的
阶沿上

Crawling Along the Lake

I crawl along the frozen lake
slipping through water weeds
far away rise cries of what sounds like a tiger.
Can they be like me
crawling over the lake
or
crossing the mountain top
over to another summit?
Lucky
the green mountain top is burning
red flames
lighting up the shiny cloud ladder
along the steep, vertical side
on edge.

我需要永远的爱

其实我需要永远的爱
不是伤害
我那心中巨大的悲情
一次又一次
高过了所有的天空
我自身在巨大的孤独中
沉静
沉静而沉静着
在喧嚣里
一切来源于我的土地
我要诉说我的诗情
给我自己
今晚我站在夜色里沉思
那来自无数友人的爱

I Want Everlasting Love

Truth is I want everlasting love,
not injury.
The enormous sadness in my heart
time and again
soars higher than the sky
and I, myself in the vast loneliness,
remain tacit.
Profound silence
in the midst of tumult
everything originates from this land.
I need to dole out my poetry
for myself.
Tonight, I stand deep in thought, well into the night
inspired by the love of many friends.

日落后

日落后
我能躺在我的小屋的椅子上
独自一人写诗
女人和孩子
都去了老屋串门子
在春日的初夜里
拉亮了屋内的灯光
伏着桌面
笔尖游动着纸声
一切静寂
这样的生活多么美好
我就是精神王国中的怪人
卡尔·斯比茨韦克的油画《穷诗人》²⁶
我在我的小屋独自写诗

After Sunset

After sunset,
I was able to lie on a chair in my little room
alone, writing poetry.
Wife and children
all went kibitzing elsewhere.
On the first spring night
I turn on the lamp
over the table
the tip of my fountain pen scratching paper
all else is quiet.
How cozy such a moment is
when I am the king of the spiritual world
like the poor poet in Spitzweg's sentimental painting.[26]
I sit in my room, alone, dreaming verses.

²⁶ 卡尔·斯比茨韦克，《穷诗人》，1839（油画，10.9市尺x 13.4市尺）。卡尔·斯比茨韦克（1808-85）德国罗曼派画家，画家风格源于彼得梅尔时期画派，主题描述日常生活场景。卡尔·斯比茨韦克自学绘画，采用佛兰芒风格进行绘画，作平以幽默，戏弄手法描述画中人物。

²⁶ Carl Spitzweg, *The Poor Poet*, 1839 (oil on canvas, 143" x 176"). Carl Spitzweg (1808—85) was a German Romantic genre painter of the Biedermeier period in art history, characterized by the depiction of everyday life through a sentimental and appreciative lens. Spitzweig was primarily self-taught and spent much of his time studying the Flemish masters. His genre paintings were beautifully rendered, playful, and sometimes plainly humorous.

天地合一

我在我的春日小院
小坐暮色中静静
天无语使人语之
地无语使人语之
这样的耳边
有风 有月 有星 有日
有花 有草 有树 有人
有乌鸦 雷声 雨声
有人语 虫声 足音
有天 有地
有暮色 有霞光
使人语之成为一器
发天地宇宙之音
四天合一 天地合一 天人合一

Four in One

Springtime in my yard
stealing a twilight moment to sit down.
Sky's silence casts into prominent relief human words
earth's silence more so.
By my ear
wind buzzes, moon, star, and sunshine
there live flower, grass, trees, and persons
there sounds rainstorm
there active worms and footsteps traverse
sky and earth.
Twilight and colorful clouds
mingling words and me in one
emitting sounds of heaven and earth
four skies in one, heaven and earth combined.

它一定就是自然的化身

我想它是一个
多么美妙的鸟儿
但是
不和我们人类亲近
今天它得了一只眼病
可以不飞不叫
沉默着
终于来找我医治
它那纤细的双脚
任意地选择着
我的手指
做为它最高贵的
栖息之地
它一定就是自然的化身

The Spirit of Nature's Reincarnation

It must be
a supernaturally beautiful bird
but
it does not endear itself to the human.
Today it contracted an eye disease
no flying, no crowing
quiet.
Finally it came to my doctor
those slim feet
choosing at will
my fingers
as its most treasured
resting place.
It must be the spirit of nature's reincarnation.

夜很深了

夜很深了
夜很深了
好似哀怨的
哭诉着
悠悠的时断时续
多少个夜
才回来了呢
哭吧 哭吧
一层叠一层
一层叠一层的
叠一层的
冬的夜好冷
我们的木头
在说话

Deep into the Dark

The night is not young.
Indeed, it is deep into the dark
as if lamenting
eternally crying
it casually hesitates.
How many nights
can recur?
Cry, let it all out
one layer after another
and more layers
on top of yet another
winter nights are so cold
our wood
is talking.

我们可否走在冬的月夜里

我们可否走在冬的月夜里
踩着僵硬的雪地
夜在天上
这个冬月十三
女儿从村外已归来
我这样想着
谁会在村子里走动
此时这里
一个空开的空间
没有夜
没有天
没有地球
在雪光和月光的交溶里
飘渺的朦胧透明中的思想

Can We Stroll on a Winter's Night?

Can we stroll on a winter's night?
Over hard-packed snow-covered ground
the night above
this winter month
my daughter returns from out of the village.
I am thinking,
Who is that walking around
at this hour?
An open space
no night
no sky
no earth
in the mix of snow and moonlight
thoughts, ethereal, hazy, transparent.

房面朝南站着

房面朝南站着
院子里围立起的葵杆　是一个长方形的菜园
窄窄的院门口　裁下了一条黄亮亮的光来.[27]
铺在房檐下的院子里
户内窗下立着闲人.
看鸡们长长的影子　在这条光里走动
看狗儿的一团黄色
在暮色里的葵杆旁蜷睡
看三五个麻雀　飞来
啄着院内的宁静
听房西旁圈内的小羊羔咩叫
听院外的落日　正在下沉
当院内一片暮色时　闲人
才在暮归的黄昏中　惊醒

---

[27] 在本诗歌集的引言部分，我谈到诗人张联用词方法。张联灵活巧妙地捉弄名词和动词字眼，在参考唐宋诗歌描述语言的同时，张联在字里行间加入日常生活用语，表现出他对中国古代诗歌的通解，也渗透出他对语言的研究。

South-Facing House

The house stands facing south
towering sunflower stalks framing a rectangular vegetable
    garden.
The gate cuts the narrow yard with a shaft of yellow light[27]
slicing a wedge of gold under the eaves.
My wife lingers inside by the window
watching the lengthening shadows of our chickens in the
    raking light
observing that ball of yellow, our dog
sound asleep by the sunflower hedge,
and she catches sight of the sparrows dipping by in the sky
pecking at the silence of the yard.
Listening to the bleating of the sheep
attending to the setting sun sinking beyond the yard
the idler lulled into a stupor
suddenly roused by twilight.

---

[27] In the introduction, I documented my discussion with the poet of his choice of words that call to attention to Tang poetry. Zhang Lian's deft manipulation of nouns and verbs that in modern Chinese are everyday usage demonstrates not only his knowledge of classical poetry but also his mastery of the modern vernacular.

Sources

Baudelaire, Charles. "Every Man His Chimæra." *The Poems and Prose Poems of Charles Baudelaire*, edited by James Huneker. Brentano's Publishers: Project Gutenberg. Retrieved June 28, 2021, from www.gutenberg.org/ebooks/36287

Bhabha, Homi, K. *The Location of Culture*. New York: Routledge, 1994.

Bio-bibliography. NobelPrize.org. Nobel Prize Outreach AB 2021. Retrieved July 3, 2021 from www.nobelprize.org/prizes/literature/2012/bio-bibliography/

Bullett, Gerald, trans. *Fan Cheng-ta: Five Seasons of a Golden Year: A Chinese Pastoral*. Hong Kong: Renditions (The Chinese University Press), 1980.

Carver, Ann C., and Sung-Sheng Yvonne Chang. *Bamboo Shoots after the Rain: Contemporary Stories by Women Writers of Taiwan*. New York: The Feminist Press at The City University of New York, 1990.

Chang, Sung-sheng. *Modernism and the Nativist Resistance: Contemporary Chinese Fiction from Taiwan*. Durham: Duke University Press, 1993.

Croll, Elisabeth J., and Huang Ping. "Migration For and Against Agriculture in Eight Chinese Villages." *The China Quarterly*, vol. 149, 1997, pp 128–146.

Empson, William. *Some Versions of Pastoral: Literary Criticism*. New York: New Directions, 1974.

Gu, Yuan-qing (古遠清). *Fin de Siècle Cultural Map of Taiwanese Literature*. Taiwan: Yang-Chih Book Co., Ltd., 2005.

Heidegger, Martin. "Building, dwelling, thinking." *Poetry, Language, Thought.* New York: Harper & Row, 1971, pp. 152–3.

Hung, Eva, ed. *Contemporary Women Writers: Hong Kong and Taiwan.* Hong Kong: Renditions (The Chinese University Press), 1990.

Idema, Wilt L., trans. *Two Centuries of Manchu Women Poets.* Seattle: University of Washington Press, 2017.

Jacobs, Andrew, and Sarah Lyall. "After Past Fury for Peace Prize, China Embraces Nobel Choice." *New York Times,* 12 Oct. 12, 2012: A1 & A5.

Keats, John. "To George and Thomas Keats (Hampstead, December 22, 1817)." *Letters of John Keats to His Family and Friends,* edited by Sidney Colvin. Project Gutenberg. Retrieved July 7, 2021 from www.gutenberg.org/ebooks/35698

Lai, Ming-yan. *Nativism and Modernity: Cultural Contestations in China and Taiwan under Global Capitalism.* Albany: State University of New York Press, 2008.

Li, Peilin, and Xiaoyi Wang, eds. *Ecological Migration, Development and Transformation: A Study of Migration and Poverty Reduction in Ningxia.* New York: Springer, 2015.

Liou, Liang-ya. *Postmodernism and Postcolonialism: Taiwanese Fiction Since 1987.* Taipei, Taiwan: Rye Field Publications, 2006.

Ma, Haiying and Lina Lian. "Rural-urban Migration and Urbanization in Gansu Province, China: Evidence from Time-series Analysis." *Asian Social Science.* Vol. 7, No. 12, 2011, pp. 141–45.

Mair, Victor H., ed. *The Columbia History of Chinese Literature.* New York: Columbia University Press, 2001.

Poggioli, Renato. *The Oaten Flute: Essays on Pastoral Poetry and the Pastoral Ideal.* Cambridge: Harvard University Press, 1975.

Said, Edward W. "The Politics of Knowledge." *Raritan* II: I (Summer 1991): 17–31.

Shiang, Yang. *The Canon of Twentieth Century Taiwan Literature (Fiction)*: *The Postwar Period, III*. Taiwan: Unitas Publishing Co., Ltd., 2006.

Theocritus. "Idylls." *The Greek Bucolic Poets*, translated by J.M. Edmonds, 1912. Cambridge: Harvard University Press, 1997, p. 47.

Wang, David Der-wei, and Carlos Rojas, eds. *Writing Taiwan: A New Literary History*. Durham: Duke University Press, 2007.

Williams, Raymond. *The Country and the City*. New York: Oxford University Press, 1973.

Xu, Xiu-zhen (許琇禎). *Comprehensive Analysis of Contemporary Taiwanese Fiction: Before and After the Martial Law, 1977–1997* (台灣當代小說縱論: 解嚴前後 1977–1997). Taipei, Taiwan: Wunan Book Publishers, 2001.

About the Translator

Keming Liu is professor of linguistics and literature, and former Chairperson of English at the City University of New York's Medgar Evers campus. An internationally recognized translator and scholar, Dr. Liu's *Voices of the Fourth Generation: China's Poets Today* (Floating World Editions, 2010) was adopted as a required text for Asian literature  courses at Hong Kong University and in the UK. It includes an historical and critical introduction to an anthology of contemporary Chinese poems that appeared in the West for the first time in English translation. Her other published works include *Adult ESL: Politics, Pedagogy, and Participation in Classroom and Community Programs* (Erlbaum, 1998), a book-length primer, *Fingertip Chinese* (Weatherhill, 2011), and a Chinese translation of Henry James's short story "Hugh Merrow" (1987). Dr. Liu's articles have appeared in *Urban Education, Geolinguistics*, and *Wadabagei*, and she covers Asian literature, linguistics, and culture as a reviewer for *Choice* magazine. Her chapter on Mo Yan, "Fiction on the Verge: Testing Taboos in The Republic of Wine," was published in *Palgrave's Handbook of Magical Realism* (2020).

Dr. Liu's work as a theorist of translation has included her doctoral seminar at St. Andrews University and her keynote address on discourse analysis and strategies at the Islands-in-Between Nineteenth International Conference convened at the University of West Indies in Barbados. She serves as the regional director of the Sino-American International Education Exchange Institute for Science and Humanities at Medgar Evers College, CUNY. Dr. Liu lives in New York City and on Long Island with her husband.

Floating World Editions

Floating World Editions publishes books that contribute to a deeper understanding of Asian cultures. Editorial supervision: Ray Furse. Book and cover design: Michelle Landry. Printing and binding: IngramSpark. The typefaces used are: Century Schoolbook, Kai, and Weibei SC.